Machine Learning for Beginners

The Definitive Guide to Neural Networks, Random Forests, and Decision Trees

Table of Contents

Introduction

Thank you for downloading Machine Learning for Beginners: *The Definitive Guide to Neural Networks, Random Forests, and Decision Trees*, and thank you for doing so. Research is continuously going on in several pet projects around universities and research centers across the world on Machine Learning. In more detail, there are different programming languages like Java, which are used in training Neural Networks. Using several languages, one can visualize all that is going on in the Neural Networks and play around with different hyper-parameter settings.

There is a growing number of people who are seeking to understand neural networks and what powers them up. To that end, the following chapters are going to discuss the algorithmic functions, methods, and code that make Neural Networks work well. You are going to follow codes that are being used to create algorithmic functions that are best used in random forests. Furthermore, you are going to see how neural networks make decisions using decision trees. This is to present algorithms in ways that will make you start out your journey in this field.

You might be tempted to jump right to the end to learn about Neural networks, but before you get there, forget about getting to learn everything at once, and focus on getting the principles that are in every chapter, so that you can gain an understanding of how the whole structure works.

There are very many books that are available in the market that explain this concept in detail, and thanks again for choosing this book. Every effort was applied to ensure that this book is useful in the understanding of the Neural network, decision trees, and random forests.

Chapter 1: MNIST Classification by the Use of Logistic Regression

We are going to start by looking at Theano or Python.

Tips on Theano

When experimenting, it is possible to engage in it for hours or even days. After the exercise, the gradient-descent can take the time to identify the appropriate parameters. Once you have determined the weights, you will need to save them, together with the estimates you will be getting, when the search continues.

Pickle is the best option if you want to save the parameters for your models. For instance, if you have shared variables, a, b, c, you will save the command like shown below:

```
>>> import cPickle
>>> save_file = open('path', 'wb')   # this will overwrite
>>> cPickle.dump(w.get_value(borrow=True), save_file, -1)
>>> cPickle.dump(v.get_value(borrow=True), save_file, -1)
>>> cPickle.dump(u.get_value(borrow=True), save_file, -1)
>>> save_file.close()
```

The data can be loaded later on like below

```
>>> save_file = open('path')
>>> w.set_value(cPickle.load(save_file), borrow=True)
>>> v.set_value(cPickle.load(save_file), borrow=True)
>>> u.set_value(cPickle.load(save_file), borrow=True)
```

This is a verbose technique which has been tried and tested. You don't need to worry because your data will be loaded and rendered in matplotlib easily, even when the aliens decide to invade earth.

No need to train functions for long term archiving

Pickle mechanisms and Python's deep-copy are compatible with Theano functions, even though the use of pickle in Theano functions should not be done. In case an update on the Theano folder is done, and any other change is done in the internal elements, then you will have a hard time to unpickle the model. Theano is on its development period, and there are expected changes in the internal APIs. If you want to be safe, your training should not be pickled in its entirety for long term storage, because it is ideal for short term storing. An example is the temp file or a copy that is made during a job distribution.

Intermediate Results plotting

To understand your models, a powerful way to interpret it is using visualizations. An insertion of PIL commands for image rendering, or plotting commands in matplotlib can be tempting. This is placed in the training script. If by any chance you see something interesting later on, on the pre-rendered images, and you find something that is not clear, you will be inclined to investigate it. By then, you will be chasing smoking mirrors because you will wish that you had saved the work.

If you have space on your hard disk, the intermediate models should be saved by the training script, and the saved models should process the visualization script.

If you are keen enough, you will notice that you have a model-saving function, and this is what you will use to save intermediate models. Consider learning more about the matplotlib, PIL which is the Python Image Library.

Now, we will show more on how Theano can implement a common classifier called the logistic regression. We will have a preview on the model's primer which is a refresher and an anchorage of the notation, and also a way to showcase the mathematical expressions on Theano graphs.

In deep ML(Machine Learning), MNIST classification problem is tackled.

The Model

A common linear classifier is the logistic-regression. The weight matrix W and a vector bias b parameterize the probabilistic classifier. An input vector is projected to a hyperplane set in order to achieve classification. Remember that each hyperplane and a particular class are directly related. The distance between the input and the hyperplanes reflects the potential that the input has in relation to a particular class.

The Theano code to be used is as follows

```
# initialize with 0 the weights W as a matrix of shape (n_in, n_out)
self.W = theano.shared(
    value=numpy.zeros(
        (n_in, n_out),
        dtype=theano.config.floatX
    ),
    name='W',
    borrow=True
)
# initialize the biases b as a vector of n_out 0s
self.b = theano.shared(
    value=numpy.zeros(
        (n_out,),
        dtype=theano.config.floatX
    ),
    name='b',
    borrow=True
)

# symbolic expression for computing the matrix of class-membership
# probabilities
# Where:
# W is a matrix where column-k represent the separation hyperplane for
# class-k
# x is a matrix where row-j  represents input training sample-j
# b is a vector where element-k represent the free parameter of
# hyperplane-k
self.p_y_given_x = T.nnet.softmax(T.dot(input, self.W) + self.b)

# symbolic description of how to compute prediction as class whose
# probability is maximal
self.y_pred = T.argmax(self.p_y_given_x, axis=1)
```

The parameters of the model have to be consistent through the entire training session; therefore, variables that are shared are allocated to W and b. This is a declaration of both variables as Theano variables that are symbolic, but the contents are also initialized. The calculation of vector P(Y |x, W, b), the Softmax operator and the dot are used. The vector-types symbolic variable is produced as p_y_given_x.

Use the T.argmax operator to find the model's actual prediction. This operator is then used to return an index that is maximal at p_y_given_x.

The code we have written does not save the world or do anything just yet; it's just a code. This is because its operators are at the initial state. We are going to learn optimal parameters.

Loss function definition

While studying optimal parameters, a loss function is an important subject to consider. In multi-class logistic-progression, negative log representation is common to be used as the loss. This is similar to likelihood maximization. It is the same as maximizing the data set D likelihood under a parameterized o for

$$\mathcal{L}(\theta = \{W, b\}, \mathcal{D}) = \sum_{i=0}^{|\mathcal{D}|} \log(P(Y = y^{(i)} | x^{(i)}, W, b))$$

$$\ell(\theta = \{W, b\}, \mathcal{D}) = -\mathcal{L}(\theta = \{W, b\}, \mathcal{D})$$

the model.

The gradient descent is a simple method that is used for minimizing nonlinear functions, compared to the more popular minimization. We are going to use stochastic gradient-method using mini-batches. Below is a Theano code that shows a minibatch loss.

```
class LogisticRegression(object):
    """Multi-class Logistic Regression Class

    The logistic regression is fully described by a weight matrix :math:`W`
    and bias vector :math:`b`. Classification is done by projecting data
    points onto a set of hyperplanes, the distance to which is used to
    determine a class membership probability.
    """

    def __init__(self, input, n_in, n_out):
        """ Initialize the parameters of the logistic regression

        :type input: theano.tensor.TensorType
        :param input: symbolic variable that describes the input of the
```

```
                architecture (one minibatch)

:type n_in: int
:param n_in: number of input units, the dimension of the space in
             which the datapoints lie

:type n_out: int
:param n_out: number of output units, the dimension of the space in
              which the labels lie

"""
# start-snippet-1
# initialize with 0 the weights W as a matrix of shape (n_in, n_out)
self.W = theano.shared(
    value=numpy.zeros(
        (n_in, n_out),
        dtype=theano.config.floatX
    ),
    name='W',
    borrow=True
)
# initialize the biases b as a vector of n_out 0s
self.b = theano.shared(
    value=numpy.zeros(
        (n_out,),
        dtype=theano.config.floatX
    ),
    name='b',
    borrow=True
)

# symbolic expression for computing the matrix of class-membership
# probabilities
# Where:
# W is a matrix where column-k represent the separation hyperplane for
# class-k
# x is a matrix where row-j  represents input training sample-j
# b is a vector where element-k represent the free parameter of
# hyperplane-k
self.p_y_given_x = T.nnet.softmax(T.dot(input, self.W) + self.b)


    # symbolic description of how to compute prediction as class whose
    # probability is maximal
    self.y_pred = T.argmax(self.p_y_given_x, axis=1)
    # end-snippet-1

    # parameters of the model
    self.params = [self.W, self.b]

    # keep track of model input
    self.input = input

def negative_log_likelihood(self, y):
```

```python
    """Return the mean of the negative log-likelihood of the prediction
    of this model under a given target distribution.

    .. math::

        \frac{1}{|\mathcal{D}|} \mathcal{L} (\theta=\{W,b\}, \mathcal{D}) =
        \frac{1}{|\mathcal{D}|} \sum_{i=0}^{|\mathcal{D}|}
            \log(P(Y=y^{(i)}|x^{(i)}, W,b)) \\
        \ell (\theta=\{W,b\}, \mathcal{D})

    :type y: theano.tensor.TensorType
    :param y: corresponds to a vector that gives for each example the
              correct label

    Note: we use the mean instead of the sum so that
          the learning rate is less dependent on the batch size
    """
    # start-snippet-2
    # y.shape[0] is (symbolically) the number of rows in y, i.e.,
    # number of examples (call it n) in the minibatch
    # T.arange(y.shape[0]) is a symbolic vector which will contain
    # [0,1,2,... n-1] T.log(self.p_y_given_x) is a matrix of
    # Log-Probabilities (call it LP) with one row per example and
    # one column per class LP[T.arange(y.shape[0]),y] is a vector
    # v containing [LP[0,y[0]], LP[1,y[1]], LP[2,y[2]], ...,
    # LP[n-1,y[n-1]]] and T.mean(LP[T.arange(y.shape[0]),y]) is
    # the mean (across minibatch examples) of the elements in v,
    # i.e., the mean log-likelihood across the minibatch.
    return -T.mean(T.log(self.p_y_given_x)[T.arange(y.shape[0]), y])
    # end-snippet-2

def errors(self, y):
    """Return a float representing the number of errors in the minibatch
    over the total number of examples of the minibatch ; zero one
    loss over the size of the minibatch


def errors(self, y):
    """Return a float representing the number of errors in the minibatch
    over the total number of examples of the minibatch ; zero one
    loss over the size of the minibatch

    :type y: theano.tensor.TensorType
    :param y: corresponds to a vector that gives for each example the
              correct label
    """

    # check if y has same dimension of y_pred
    if y.ndim != self.y_pred.ndim:
        raise TypeError(
            'y should have the same shape as self.y_pred',
            ('y', y.type, 'y_pred', self.y_pred.type)
        )
    # check if y is of the correct datatype
    if y.dtype.startswith('int'):
        # the T.neq operator returns a vector of 0s and 1s, where 1
        # represents a mistake in prediction
        return T.mean(T.neq(self.y_pred, y))
    else:
```

Chapter 2: Multi-Layer Perception (MLP)

This is the next architecture that is presented by Theano. A Multi-Layer Perception can also be identified like a classifier in logistic regression; this is because there is a transformation of the input that is transformed by the use of a learned nonlinear transformation. There is a projection of the input data to a space using transformation projects, which makes it become separable linearly. The hidden layer is what is used to describe an intermediate layer. MLPs can be **universal approximators** by the use of one hidden layer.

The Model

The diagram below shows one layer hidden neural network.

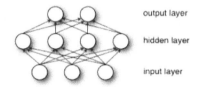

output layer

hidden layer

input layer

Ideally, a layer of hidden is represented by a function $f : R^D \to R^L$, where D is the same as the x vector, in size. L's the same as vector output $f(x)$, because, when you look at the matrix notation,

$$f(x) = G(b^{(2)} + W^{(2)}(s(b^{(1)} + W^{(1)}x))).$$

Has $b^{(1)}$ and $b^{(2)}$ as bias vectors; matrices as weight $W^{(1)}$, $W^{(2)}$ then G and s as activation functions.

Vector $h(x) = \Phi(x) = s(b^{(1)} + W^{(1)}x)$ has a layer that is hidden. $W^{(1)} \in R^{D \times D_h}$

This represents a weight matrix that is connected to both the hidden layer and the input vector. Every single column $W^{(1)}_{\cdot i}$ is a representation of the weights that go to the i-th unit that is hidden, from the input units. The choices that are available for *s* include *tanh, with tanh(a)=(e^a-e^-a)/(e^a+e^-a)*, or the *sigmoid* function, that has sigmoid(a)=1/(1+e^-a). Tanh will be used since it yields better local maxima and faster training. Sigmoid and Tanh are scalar-to-scalar functions, but the tensors and vectors in their natural extension consist when applied elementary. For instance, separating each vectors element, achieving a vector that is of the same size.

Then, $o(x) = G(b^{(2)} + W^{(2)}h(x))$ is the vectors output. Keep in mind that the form used in MNIST classification digits using Logistic Regression in chapter 1. Obtaining of class membership probabilities is possible using *G* which is the *Softmax* function.

In MLP training, all model parameters are learned, and SGD (Stoch-Gradient Descent) is used with mini batches. The set $\theta = \{W^{(2)}, b^{(2)}, W^{(1)}, b^{(1)}\}$ is the one that is used in learning. Backpropagation algorithm can be obtained through. The good thing is that Theano does differentiation automatically.

Heading to MPL from logistic regression

We are going to focus on MLP hidden layer. A class representation of a hidden layer is started. To have the MLP constructed, there has to be a layer of logistic regression at the top.

```
class HiddenLayer(object):
    def __init__(self, rng, input, n_in, n_out, W=None, b=None,
                    activation=T.tanh):
"""
```

An MLP hidden layer: fully-connected units and have
activation functions for sigmoid. W Weight matrix having the shape (n_out, n_in,)
and b which is the bias vector of (n_out,) shape.
NOTE: The nonlinearity used here is tanh
tanh(dot(input,W) + b) provides the activation that is hidden
:type rng: numpy.random.RandomState
:param rng: a generator that produces random numbers that initialize weights
:type input: theano.tensor.dmatrix
:param input: a symbolic tensor of shape (n_examples, n_in)
:type n_in: int

:param n_in: dimensionality of input
:type n_out: int

:param n_out: no. of units that are hidden
:type activation: theano.Op or function
:param activation: hidden layer to use Nonlinearity
"""

self.input = input

The initial weights value of the hidden layer needs to be sampled uniformly from an interval that is dependent and symmetric on the activation function. Initialization makes certain that when training is in progress, every single neuron function that is in its activation function allows propagation of information in both upwards and downwards direction. When we talk about upwards, we mean that there is a flow of activation from the input to the output. On the contrary, a backward propagation means that the gradient flows from the output to the inputs.

Theoretically, the graph is implemented by the graph that calculates the value of the hidden layer $h(x) = \Phi(x) = s(b^{(1)} + W^{(1)}x)$. If this graph is used in the *Logistic Regression class* as an input, it is then implemented in the MNIST classification logistic Regression, as the MLP becomes the output. The following MLP class short implementation is described below.

```
class MLP(object):
    """Multi-Layer Perceptron Class

    A multilayer perceptron is a feedforward artificial neural network model
    that has one layer or more of hidden units and nonlinear activations.
    Intermediate layers usually have as activation function tanh or the
    sigmoid function (defined here by a ''HiddenLayer'' class) while the
    top layer is a softmax layer (defined here by a ''LogisticRegression''
    class).
    """

    def __init__(self, rng, input, n_in, n_hidden, n_out):
        """Initialize the parameters for the multilayer perceptron

        :type rng: numpy.random.RandomState
        :param rng: a random number generator used to initialize weights

        :type input: theano.tensor.TensorType
        :param input: symbolic variable that describes the input of the
        architecture (one minibatch)

        :type n_in: int
        :param n_in: number of input units, the dimension of the space in
        which the datapoints lie

        :type n_hidden: int
        :param n_hidden: number of hidden units

        :type n_out: int
        :param n_out: number of output units, the dimension of the space in
        which the labels lie

        """

        # Since we are dealing with a one hidden layer MLP, this will translate
        # into a HiddenLayer with a tanh activation function connected to the
        # LogisticRegression layer; the activation function can be replaced by
        # sigmoid or any other nonlinear function
        self.hiddenLayer = HiddenLayer(
            rng=rng,
            input=input,
            n_in=n_in,

            n_out=n_hidden,
            activation=T.tanh
        )

        # The logistic regression layer gets as input the hidden units
        # of the hidden layer
        self.logRegressionLayer = LogisticRegression(
            input=self.hiddenLayer.output,
            n_in=n_hidden,
            n_out=n_out
        )
```

We are also going to use regularization of L1 and L2, and we are also going to
calculate the norm L1 and the norm L2 of $W^{(1)}$, $W^{(2)}$.

```
# LI norm ; one regularization option is to enforce LI norm to
# be small
self.L1 = (
    abs(self.hiddenLayer.W).sum()
    + abs(self.logRegressionLayer.W).sum()
)

# square of LI norm ; one regularization option is to enforce
# square of LI norm to be small
self.L2_sqr = (
    (self.hiddenLayer.W ** 2).sum()
    + (self.logRegressionLayer.W ** 2).sum()
)

# negative log likelihood of the MLP is given by the negative
# log likelihood of the output of the model, computed in the
# logistic regression layer
self.negative_log_likelihood = (
    self.logRegressionLayer.negative_log_likelihood
)
# same holds for the function computing the number of errors
self.errors = self.logRegressionLayer.errors

# the parameters of the model are the parameters of the two layer it is
# made out of
self.params = self.hiddenLayer.params + self.logRegressionLayer.params
```

The model is then trained by the use of stochastic-gradient-descent with the help of mini-batches. The main difference comes in cost function modification so that there is the inclusion of regularization. L1_reg and L2_REG control the terms of regularization in the function of the total cost. The new cost code is as below:

```
# the cost we minimize during training is the negative log likelihood of
# the model plus the regularization terms (L1 and L2); cost is expressed
# here symbolically
cost = (
    classifier.negative_log_likelihood(y)
    + L1_reg * classifier.L1
```

The gradient is then used to update the model. The code comes close to imitate the logistic regression's code, with the number of parameters causing the difference. In order to hack this difference, we are going to be like Superman, use our super strength to pull the two worlds together. Well, that's a wild wish; what we are going to do, is to write a code that will allow any number of parameters to work. Using the parameters list that we developed earlier, and parse the params model, and then compute each steps gradient.

```
# compute the gradient of cost with respect to theta (sotred in params)
# the resulting gradients will be stored in a list gparams
gparams = [T.grad(cost, param) for param in classifier.params]

# specify how to update the parameters of the model as a list of
# (variable, update expression) pairs

# given two lists of the same length, A = [a1, a2, a3, a4] and
# B = [b1, b2, b3, b4], zip generates a list C of same size, where each
# element is a pair formed from the two lists :
#     C = [(a1, b1), (a2, b2), (a3, b3), (a4, b4)]
updates = [
    (param, param - learning_rate * gparam)
    for param, gparam in zip(classifier.params, gparams)
]

# compiling a Theano function 'train_model' that returns the cost, but
# in the same time updates the parameter of the model based on the rules
# defined in 'updates'
train_model = theano.function(
    inputs=[index],
    outputs=cost,
    updates=updates,
    givens={
        x: train_set_x[index * batch_size: (index + 1) * batch_size],
        y: train_set_y[index * batch_size: (index + 1) * batch_size]
    }
)
```

Condensation of the points

We have looked into the basic concepts that can help one to easily write an
MLP. We are going to look at how this is done, in a way that is analogous to
the implementation of the logistic regression seen previously.

```
"""
This tutorial introduces the multilayer perceptron using Theano.

A multilayer perceptron is a logistic regressor where
instead of feeding the input to the logistic regression you insert a
intermediate layer, called the hidden layer, that has a nonlinear
activation function (usually tanh or sigmoid) . One can use many such
hidden layers making the architecture deep. The tutorial will also tackle
the problem of MNIST digit classification.
```

.. math::

    f(x) = G(b^{(2)} + W^{(2)}(s(b^{(1)} + W^{(1)} x))),

References:

    - textbooks: "Pattern Recognition and Machine Learning" -
                 Christopher M. Bishop, section 5

"""
__docformat__ = 'restructedtext en'

import os
import sys
import timeit

import numpy

import theano
import theano.tensor as T

from logistic_sgd import LogisticRegression, load_data

# start-snippet-1
class HiddenLayer(object):
    def __init__(self, rng, input, n_in, n_out, W=None, b=None,
                 activation=T.tanh):
        """
        Typical hidden layer of a MLP: units are fully-connected and have
        sigmoidal activation function. Weight matrix W is of shape (n_in,n_o
        and the bias vector b is of shape (n_out,).

        NOTE : The nonlinearity used here is tanh

        Hidden unit activation is given by: tanh(dot(input,W) + b)

        :type rng: numpy.random.RandomState
        :param rng: a random number generator used to initialize weights

        :type input: theano.tensor.dmatrix
        :param input: a symbolic tensor of shape (n_examples, n_in)

        :type n_in: int
        :param n_in: dimensionality of input

        :type n_out: int
        :param n_out: number of hidden units

        :type activation: theano.Op or function
        :param activation: Non linearity to be applied in the hidden
```
```

```python
                            layer
        """
        self.input = input
        # end-snippet-1

        # `W` is initialized with `W_values` which is uniformly sampled
        # from sqrt(-6./(n_in+n_hidden)) and sqrt(6./(n_in+n_hidden))
        # for tanh activation function
        # the output of uniform if converted using asarray to dtype
        # theano.config.floatX so that the code is runable on GPU
        # Note : optimal initialization of weights is dependent on the
        #        activation function used (among other things).
        #        For example, results presented in [Xavier10] suggest that you
        #        should use 4 times larger initial weights for sigmoid
        #        compared to tanh
        #        We have no info for other function, so we use the same as
        #        tanh.
        if W is None:
            W_values = numpy.asarray(
                rng.uniform(
                    low=-numpy.sqrt(6. / (n_in + n_out)),
                    high=numpy.sqrt(6. / (n_in + n_out)),
                    size=(n_in, n_out)
                ),
                dtype=theano.config.floatX
            )
            if activation == theano.tensor.nnet.sigmoid:
                W_values *= 4

            W = theano.shared(value=W_values, name='W', borrow=True)

        if b is None:
            b_values = numpy.zeros((n_out,), dtype=theano.config.floatX)
            b = theano.shared(value=b_values, name='b', borrow=True)

        self.W = W
        self.b = b

        lin_output = T.dot(input, self.W) + self.b
        self.output = (
            lin_output if activation is None
            else activation(lin_output)
        )
        # parameters of the model
        self.params = [self.W, self.b]


# start-snippet-2
class MLP(object):
    """Multi-Layer Perceptron Class

    A multilayer perceptron is a feedforward artificial neural network model
    that has one layer or more of hidden units and nonlinear activations.
```

Intermediate layers usually have as activation function tanh or the
sigmoid function (defined here by a ``HiddenLayer`` class) while the
top layer is a softmax layer (defined here by a ``LogisticRegression``
class).
"""

def __init__(self, rng, input, n_in, n_hidden, n_out):
    """Initialize the parameters for the multilayer perceptron

    :type rng: numpy.random.RandomState
    :param rng: a random number generator used to initialize weights

    :type input: theano.tensor.TensorType
    :param input: symbolic variable that describes the input of the
    architecture (one minibatch)

    :type n_in: int
    :param n_in: number of input units, the dimension of the space in
    which the datapoints lie

    :type n_hidden: int
    :param n_hidden: number of hidden units

    :type n_out: int
    :param n_out: number of output units, the dimension of the space in
    which the labels lie

    """

    # Since we are dealing with a one hidden layer MLP, this will translate
    # into a HiddenLayer with a tanh activation function connected to the
    # LogisticRegression layer; the activation function can be replaced by
    # sigmoid or any other nonlinear function
    self.hiddenLayer = HiddenLayer(
        rng=rng,
        input=input,
        n_in=n_in,
        n_out=n_hidden,
        activation=T.tanh
)

    # The logistic regression layer gets as input the hidden units
    # of the hidden layer
    self.logRegressionLayer = LogisticRegression(
        input=self.hiddenLayer.output,
        n_in=n_hidden,
        n_out=n_out
)
    # end-snippet-2 start-snippet-3
    # L1 norm ; one regularization option is to enforce L1 norm to
    # be small
    self.L1 = (
        abs(self.hiddenLayer.W).sum()

```python
            + abs(self.logRegressionLayer.W).sum()
        )

        # square of L2 norm ; one regularization option is to enforce
        # square of L2 norm to be small
        self.L2_sqr = (
            (self.hiddenLayer.W ** 2).sum()
            + (self.logRegressionLayer.W ** 2).sum()
        )

        # negative log likelihood of the MLP is given by the negative
        # log likelihood of the output of the model, computed in the
        # logistic regression layer
        self.negative_log_likelihood = (
            self.logRegressionLayer.negative_log_likelihood
        )
        # same holds for the function computing the number of errors
        self.errors = self.logRegressionLayer.errors

        # the parameters of the model are the parameters of the two layer it is
        # made out of
        self.params = self.hiddenLayer.params + self.logRegressionLayer.params
        # end-snippet-3

        # keep track of model input
        self.input = input


def test_mlp(learning_rate=0.01, L1_reg=0.00, L2_reg=0.0001, n_epochs=1000,
             dataset='mnist.pkl.gz', batch_size=20, n_hidden=500):
    """
    Demonstrate stochastic gradient descent optimization for a multilayer
    perceptron

    This is demonstrated on MNIST.

    :type learning_rate: float
    :param learning_rate: learning rate used (factor for the stochastic
    gradient)

    :type L1_reg: float
    :param L1_reg: L1-norm's weight when added to the cost (see
    regularization)

    :type L2_reg: float
    :param L2_reg: L2-norm's weight when added to the cost (see
    regularization)

    :type n_epochs: int
    :param n_epochs: maximal number of epochs to run the optimizer

    :type dataset: string
    :param dataset: the path of the MNIST dataset file from
```

```
"""

datasets = load_data(dataset)

train_set_x, train_set_y = datasets[0]
valid_set_x, valid_set_y = datasets[1]
test_set_x, test_set_y = datasets[2]

# compute number of minibatches for training, validation and testing
n_train_batches = train_set_x.get_value(borrow=True).shape[0] / batch_size
n_valid_batches = valid_set_x.get_value(borrow=True).shape[0] / batch_size
n_test_batches = test_set_x.get_value(borrow=True).shape[0] / batch_size

########################
# BUILD ACTUAL MODEL #
########################
print '... building the model'

# allocate symbolic variables for the data
index = T.lscalar()  # index to a [minibatch]
x = T.matrix('x')  # the data is presented as rasterized images
y = T.ivector('y')  # the labels are presented as 1D vector of
                    # [int] labels

rng = numpy.random.RandomState(1234)

# construct the MLP class
classifier = MLP(
    rng=rng,
    input=x,
    n_in=28 * 28,
    n_hidden=n_hidden,
    n_out=10
)

# start-snippet-4
# the cost we minimize during training is the negative log likelihood of
# the model plus the regularization terms (L1 and L2); cost is expressed
# here symbolically
cost = (
    classifier.negative_log_likelihood(y)
    + L1_reg * classifier.L1
    + L2_reg * classifier.L2_sqr
)
# end-snippet-4

# compiling a Theano function that computes the mistakes that are made
# by the model on a minibatch
test_model = theano.function(
    inputs=[index],
    outputs=classifier.errors(y),
```

```python
    givens={
        x: test_set_x[index * batch_size:(index + 1) * batch_size],
        y: test_set_y[index * batch_size:(index + 1) * batch_size]
    }
)

validate_model = theano.function(
    inputs=[index],
    outputs=classifier.errors(y),
    givens={
        x: valid_set_x[index * batch_size:(index + 1) * batch_size],
        y: valid_set_y[index * batch_size:(index + 1) * batch_size]
    }
)

# start-snippet-5
# compute the gradient of cost with respect to theta (sotred in params)
# the resulting gradients will be stored in a list gparams
gparams = [T.grad(cost, param) for param in classifier.params]

# specify how to update the parameters of the model as a list of
# (variable, update expression) pairs

# given two lists of the same length, A = [a1, a2, a3, a4] and
# B = [b1, b2, b3, b4], zip generates a list C of same size, where each
# element is a pair formed from the two lists :
#    C = [(a1, b1), (a2, b2), (a3, b3), (a4, b4)]
updates = [
    (param, param - learning_rate * gparam)
    for param, gparam in zip(classifier.params, gparams)
]

# compiling a Theano function 'train_model' that returns the cost, but
# in the same time updates the parameter of the model based on the rules
# defined in 'updates'
train_model = theano.function(
    inputs=[index],
    outputs=cost,
    updates=updates,
    givens={
        x: train_set_x[index * batch_size: (index + 1) * batch_size],
        y: train_set_y[index * batch_size: (index + 1) * batch_size]
    }
)
# end-snippet-5

###############
# TRAIN MODEL #
###############
print '... training'

# early-stopping parameters
patience = 10000  # look as this many examples regardless
```

```python
patience_increase = 2  # wait this much longer when a new best is
                       # found
improvement_threshold = 0.995  # a relative improvement of this much is
                               # considered significant
validation_frequency = min(n_train_batches, patience / 2)
                               # go through this many
                               # minibatche before checking the network
                               # on the validation set; in this case we
                               # check every epoch

best_validation_loss = numpy.inf
best_iter = 0
test_score = 0.
start_time = timeit.default_timer()

epoch = 0
done_looping = False

while (epoch < n_epochs) and (not done_looping):
    epoch = epoch + 1
    for minibatch_index in xrange(n_train_batches):

        minibatch_avg_cost = train_model(minibatch_index)
        # iteration number
        iter = (epoch - 1) * n_train_batches + minibatch_index

        if (iter + 1) % validation_frequency == 0:
            # compute zero-one loss on validation set
            validation_losses = [validate_model(i) for i
                                 in xrange(n_valid_batches)]
            this_validation_loss = numpy.mean(validation_losses)

            print(
                'epoch %i, minibatch %i/%i, validation error %f %%' %
                (
                    epoch,
                    minibatch_index + 1,
                    n_train_batches,
                    this_validation_loss * 100.
                )
            )

            # if we got the best validation score until now
            if this_validation_loss < best_validation_loss:
                #improve patience if loss improvement is good enough
                if (
                    this_validation_loss < best_validation_loss *
                    improvement_threshold
                ):
                    patience = max(patience, iter * patience_increase)

                best_validation_loss = this_validation_loss
                best_iter = iter
```

```
        # test it on the test set
        test_losses = [test_model(i) for i
                          in xrange(n_test_batches)]
        test_score = numpy.mean(test_losses)

        print(('     epoch %i, minibatch %i/%i, test error of '
               'best model %f %%') %
              (epoch, minibatch_index + 1, n_train_batches,
               test_score * 100.))

        if patience <= iter:
            done_looping = True
            break

    end_time = timeit.default_timer()
    print(('Optimization complete. Best validation score of %f %% '
           'obtained at iteration %i, with test performance %f %%') %
          (best_validation_loss * 100., best_iter + 1, test_score * 100.))
    print >> sys.stderr, ('The code for file ' +
                          os.path.split(__file__)[1] +
                          ' ran for %.2fm' % ((end_time - start_time) / 60.))


if __name__ == '__main__':
    test_mlp()
```

The user can then run the code by calling :

```
python code/mlp.py
```

The output one should expect is of the form :

```
Optimization complete. Best validation score of 1.690000 % obtained at iteration 2070000,
The code for file mlp.py ran for 97.34m
```

On an Intel(R) Core(TM) i7-2600K CPU @ 3.40GHz the code runs with approximately 10.3 epoch/minute and it took 828 epochs to reach a test error of 1.65%.

Chapter 3: Convolutional Neural Networks

This chapter can be understood well after the first two chapters have been read. We are going to use new functions of Theano and the concepts: shared Variables, downsample, T.grad, conv2d floatX, dimshuffle and basic arithmetic ops. A good GPU is needed to run this, with at least a 1GB RAM. If you have connected your monitor to the GPU, then you may need a bigger RAM size. This is because, if the GPU is hooked to your monitor, each GPU function call will take some seconds as a limit when calling a function in the GPU. If this limit would not be present, you will witness a lot of screen hanging or freezing for a long time. But if you have not connected your GPU to the monitor, then you won't have any time limit. If you experience a timeout issue, you will only lower the size of the batch and you are good to go.

Motivation

One Neural Network variant of the MLP that is referred to as Convolutional is inspired biologically. In a study of the neural cortex of a cat, it was discovered that the visual cortex has an intricate cells arrangement. The cells are very sensitive to minute sub-regions of the visual field that is referred to as a receptive field. The whole visual field is covered and the cells represent local filters that are designed to take advantage of the natural images local correlation.

There are types of cells which have been discovered; the cells types in question are what we call complex and simple cells.

Simple: they are responsive to edge-like-patterns that are in their receptive fields.

Complex: these cells have a larger field of reception which are invariant to the patterns definite position. The most powerful visual cortex is the animal visual cortex. This is because it has an amazing processing system, which is the best example to learn from. This has made many models of neural networks to be designed in the literature. Some of the most common inspired-models are LeNET-5, HMAX, and Neocognitron.

Sparse Connectivity

CNN's enforce a local connectivity pattern between layers that are adjacent and neurons, to exploit the spatially-local-correlation. This means that the hidden input units in the m layer originate from unit subsets of layer m-1 that possess receptive fields that are spatially contiguous. To view it graphically, check out the diagram below:

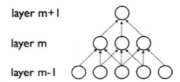

Consider layer m-1 being the input of retina. Using the figure above, **m's** layer input has fields that are receptive. These fields have width three in the input of the retina, and they are linked to three neurons that are located adjacent to each other in the retina. Layer m+1 units have the same kind of connection as the one below. Their receptive-field has 3 concerning the layer that follows. But if you look at the receptive field compared to the input, it's larger. Outside the field of reception, the units are not responsive to variations that are related with the retina. The learned filters are taken care of by the architecture to produce strong responses to an input pattern that is local.

Like it has been seen above, the stacking of layers like this makes it ideal for filters that become global. For instance, the hidden layers **m+1** units can encode a nonlinear 5 width pixel space.

Shared Weights

Each filter in CNN is duplicated across the whole visual field. These units that have been duplicated have similar parameterization, forming a *feature map*.

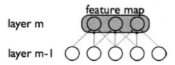

In the figure above, there are three units that are hidden that belong to one feature map. The same weights have the same color. Shared parameters can be learned by the gradient descent, with a minute change to the algorithm. The gradients sum of the parameters is what is called the shared weight's gradient. CNNs are enabled to get better vision generalization by the use of constraints.

Details and Notation

A repeated application of the sub-regions functions of the whole image obtains a feature map. This means that the input image convolution uses a linear filter, adds a bias term and applies a nonlinear-function. If k-th in a feature map is denoted at a selected given layer as h^k, and the filters are done by weights W^k, and b_k bias, then h^k, which is the feature map is obtained using:

$$h_{ij}^k = \tanh((W^k * x)_{ij} + b_k).$$

To have a more detailed data representation, several feature maps are in every hidden layer, $\{h^{(k)}, k=0..K\}$. Each hidden layer Weights W can be represented in a containing element of a 4D-tensor. This is for each collection of the following maps(source-feature and destination-feature) together with source positions, horizontal and vertical. Using a vector that has an element for each destination-feature-map, there can be a representation of the biases b. Graphically, we can represent this as below:

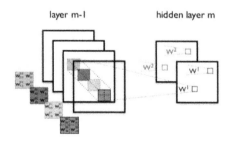

This is a representation of two VNN layers. We have Layer **m-1** which has 4 feature maps. Then we have the Hidden-layer **m** which has 2 feature maps (h^1 and h^o). The neuron outputs that are in h^1 and h^o, that are visible in red and blue squares, are calculated from the layer **m-1** that is in their 2x2 receptive field. You should take note of how the receptive field covers the feature map inputs. Weights W^o & W^1 of h^o and h^1 are tensors of 3D weight. The input feature-maps are indexed by the leading dimension, while the pixel coordinates are referred to the other two.

When you summarize it all, W^{kl}_{ij} represents each pixel's weight connection of the maps k-th feature when you look at the m layer, while having the coordinates of the pixel at (i,j) on the layer(m-1) of the l-th feature map.

Convolution Operator

The main workhorse is the ConvOp that is used to implement Theanos convolutional layer. ConvOp is utilized by theano.tensor.signal.conv2d that takes 2 inputs that are symbolic. There are two inputs that are taken by these, which are:

- A 4D tensor that corresponds to input images that are mini batch. The tensors shape is identified by [image height, mini-batch size, image width, no.of feature input maps]

- A 4D tensor that corresponds to weight matrix W. The tensors shape is: [no.of feature maps that are at layer m, filter width, filter height, no.of features at layer m-1]

Let us look at the Theano code that implements a convolutional layer. There are 3-feature maps that are of 120x160 size. 2 convolutional filters that have 9x9 receptive fields are used.

```python
import theano
from theano import tensor as T
from theano.tensor.nnet import conv

import numpy

rng = numpy.random.RandomState(23455)

# instantiate 4D tensor for input
input = T.tensor4(name='input')

# initialize shared variable for weights.
w_shp = (2, 3, 9, 9)
w_bound = numpy.sqrt(3 * 9 * 9)
W = theano.shared( numpy.asarray(
            rng.uniform(
                low=-1.0 / w_bound,
                high=1.0 / w_bound,
                size=w_shp),
            dtype=input.dtype), name ='W')

# initialize shared variable for bias (1D tensor) with random values
# IMPORTANT: biases are usually initialized to zero. However in this
# particular application, we simply apply the convolutional layer to
# an image without learning the parameters. We therefore initialize
# them to random values to "simulate" learning.
b_shp = (2,)
b = theano.shared(numpy.asarray(
            rng.uniform(low=-.5, high=.5, size=b_shp),
            dtype=input.dtype), name ='b')
```

```
# build symbolic expression that computes the convolution of input wit
conv_out = conv.conv2d(input, W)

# build symbolic expression to add bias and apply activation function,
# A few words on ''dimshuffle'' :
#    ''dimshuffle'' is a powerful tool in reshaping a tensor;
#    what it allows you to do is to shuffle dimension around
#    but also to insert new ones along which the tensor will be
#    broadcastable;
#    dimshuffle('x', 2, 'x', 0, 1)
#    This will work on 3d tensors with no broadcastable
#    dimensions. The first dimension will be broadcastable,
#    then we will have the third dimension of the input tensor as
#    the second of the resulting tensor, etc. If the tensor has
#    shape (20, 30, 40), the resulting tensor will have dimensions
#    (1, 40, 1, 20, 30). (AxBxC tensor is mapped to 1xCx1xAxB tensor)
#    More examples:
#    dimshuffle('x') -> make a 0d (scalar) into a 1d vector
#    dimshuffle(0, 1) -> identity
#    dimshuffle(1, 0) -> inverts the first and second dimensions
#    dimshuffle('x', 0) -> make a row out of a 1d vector (N to 1xN)
#    dimshuffle(0, 'x') -> make a column out of a 1d vector (N to Nx1)
#    dimshuffle(2, 0, 1) -> AxBxC to CxAxB
#    dimshuffle(0, 'x', 1) -> AxB to Ax1xB
#    dimshuffle(1, 'x', 0) -> AxB to Bx1xA
output = T.nnet.sigmoid(conv_out + b.dimshuffle('x', 0, 'x', 'x'))

# create theano function to compute filtered images
f = theano.function([input], output)
```

Let's dig in and have some fun

```
import numpy
import pylab
from PIL import Image

# open random image of dimensions 639x516
img = Image.open(open('doc/images/3wolfmoon.jpg'))
# dimensions are (height, width, channel)
img = numpy.asarray(img, dtype='float64') / 256.

# put image in 4D tensor of shape (1, 3, height, width)
img_ = img.transpose(2, 0, 1).reshape(1, 3, 639, 516)
filtered_img = f(img_)

# plot original image and first and second components of output
pylab.subplot(1, 3, 1); pylab.axis('off'); pylab.imshow(img)
pylab.gray();
# recall that the convOp output (filtered image) is actually a "minibatch",
# of size 1 here, so we take index 0 in the first dimension:
pylab.subplot(1, 3, 2); pylab.axis('off');
pylab.imshow(filtered_img[0, 0, :, :])
pylab.subplot(1, 3, 3); pylab.axis('off');
pylab.imshow(filtered_img[0, 1, :, :])

pylab.show()
```

Below is the expected generated output

You should notice that a random initialized filter is the one that behaves like edge detectors. The same weight initialization formula has been used with MLP. There is a random sampling of the weights from a distribution that is uniform, which ranges from $[-1/\text{fan-in}$, to $1/\text{fan-in}]$.Here, fan-in represents the unit-inputs that are hidden. In Multi-Layer Perceptions, it looks into the layer below and represents the units in it. When you go to CNN, you need to consider the input features, together with the size of the receptive field.

Max Pooling

Max Pooling is one important concept in CNN that is a nonlinear form of down-sampling. Max pooling segments input images to rectangular non-overlapping sets, and when you look at each sub-region, the max value is yielded as an output.

Vision benefits from max-pooling because of 2 simple reasons

- It eliminates values that are non-maximal, reducing upper layer computation.

- A translation invariance is provided. Think about cascading a max pool layer using a convolution layer;it's a sight for sore eyes. One can translate input images in eight different directions using just one pixel. When max pooling is implemented on a 2x2 region, three of the eight configurations that are possible produce the same convolutional layer output. When max pooling goes to 3x3, it jumps to 5/8.

- Since additional robustness is provided, max pooling is an efficient way of reducing intermediate representations dimensionality.

- Max-pooling in Theano is done by theano.tensor.signal.downsample.max_pool_2d/ an N dimensional tensor is taken as an input. It is also taken as a downscaling factor that does max pooling over the 2 trailing tensor dimensions.

You might have gotten lost in the explanation, but not to worry. If you understand coding much more, then here is your pie!

```
from theano.tensor.signal import downsample

input = T.dtensor4('input')
maxpool_shape = (2, 2)
pool_out = downsample.max_pool_2d(input, maxpool_shape,

ignore_border=True)

f = theano.function([input],pool_out)

invals = numpy.random.RandomState(1).rand(3, 2, 5, 5)


print 'With ignore_border set to True:'
print 'invals[0, 0, :, :] =\n', invals[0, 0, :, :]
print 'output[0, 0, :, :] =\n', f(invals)[0, 0, :, :]

pool_out = downsample.max_pool_2d(input, maxpool_shape,

ignore_border=False)

f = theano.function([input],pool_out)
print 'With ignore_border set to False:'
print 'invals[1, 0, :, :] =\n ', invals[1, 0, :, :]
print 'output[1, 0, :, :] =\n ', f(invals)[1, 0, :, :]
```

The following output should be generated:

```
With ignore_border set to True:
    invals[0, 0, :, :] =
    [[ 4.17022005e-01   7.20324493e-01   1.14374817e-04
     [ 9.23385948e-02   1.86260211e-01   3.45560727e-01
     [ 4.19194514e-01   6.85219500e-01   2.04452250e-01
     [ 6.70467510e-01   4.17304802e-01   5.58689828e-01
     [ 8.00744569e-01   9.68261576e-01   3.13424178e-01
```

Below is a continuation of the invals that should complete the rows

```
  3.02332573e-01 1.46755891e-01]
  3.96767474e-01 5.38816734e-01]
  8.78117436e-01 2.73875932e-02]
  1.40386939e-01 1.98101489e-01]
  6.92322616e-01 8.76389152e-01]]

output[0, 0, :, :] =
 [[ 0.72032449  0.39676747]
  [ 0.6852195   0.87811744]]


With ignore_border set to False:
    invals[1, 0, :, :] =
     [[ 0.01936696  0.67883553  0.21162812  0.26554666  0.49157316]
      [ 0.05336255  0.57411761  0.14672857  0.58930554  0.69975836]
      [ 0.10233443  0.41405599  0.69440016  0.41417927  0.04995346]
      [ 0.53589641  0.66379465  0.51488911  0.94459476  0.58655504]
      [ 0.90340192  0.1374747   0.13927635  0.80739129  0.39767684]]
    output[1, 0, :, :] =
     [[ 0.67883553  0.58930554  0.69975836]
      [ 0.66379465  0.94459476  0.58655504]
      [ 0.90340192  0.80739129  0.39767684]]
```

If you compare it to most codes of Theano, the max_pool_2d is special. The downscaling factor is required, represented by *ds* which will be known in the graph building. This changes as we carry on.

LeNet: The Full Model

Convolutional layers, Sparse, and max-pooling are usually central in LeNet models. The modular details vary; you can use the diagram below to see the pictorial representation of the LeNet model.

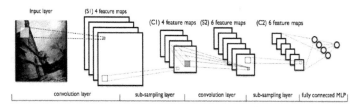

Max-pooling and convolution are what constitutes the lower layers. A traditional MLP which comprises of the logistic regression and the hidden layer is what the upper layer corresponds and fully connects to. The layer below that has all the feature maps has the input set to the 1st fully connected layer.

When you look at the implementation perspective, layers that are on the low work on tensors that are 4D. A 2 Dimensional matrix is achieved after the 4-dimensional matrix is flattened, forming feature maps that are rasterized, and that are compatible to the MLP that was previously implemented.

Summary by combining it all

A LeNet model is now easy to implement since we have all we need. To start us off, we use the LeNetConvPoolLayer class that implements the max-pool and convolution layer.

```
class LeNetConvPoolLayer(object):
    """Pool Layer of a convolutional network """

    def __init__(self, rng, input, filter_shape, image_shape,
poolsize=(2, 2)):
     Allocate a LeNetConvPoolLayer with shared variable internal parameters.
     :type rng: numpy.random.RandomState
     :param rng: a random number generator used to initialize weights

     :type input: theano.tensor.dtensor4
     :param input: symbolic image tensor, of shape image_shape

     :type filter_shape: tuple or list of length 4
     :param filter_shape: (number of filters, num input feature maps,
                            filter height, filter width)

     :type image_shape: tuple or list of length 4
     :param image_shape: (batch size, num input feature maps,
                           image height, image width)

     :type poolsize: tuple or list of length 2
     :param poolsize: the downsampling (pooling) factor (#rows, #cols)
     """
```

```
assert image_shape[1] == filter_shape[1]
self.input = input

# there are "num input feature maps * filter height * filter width"
# inputs to each hidden unit
fan_in = numpy.prod(filter_shape[1:])
# each unit in the lower layer receives a gradient from:
# "num output feature maps * filter height * filter width" /
#   pooling size
fan_out = (filter_shape[0] * numpy.prod(filter_shape[2:]) /
            numpy.prod(poolsize))
# initialize weights with random weights
W_bound = numpy.sqrt(6. / (fan_in + fan_out))
self.W = theano.shared(
    numpy.asarray(
        rng.uniform(low=-W_bound, high=W_bound, size=filter_shape),
        dtype=theano.config.floatX
    ),
    borrow=True
)

# the bias is a 1D tensor -- one bias per output feature map
b_values = numpy.zeros((filter_shape[0],), dtype=theano.config.floatX)
self.b = theano.shared(value=b_values, borrow=True)

# convolve input feature maps with filters
conv_out = conv.conv2d(
    input=input,
    filters=self.W,
    filter_shape=filter_shape,
    image_shape=image_shape
)

# downsample each feature map individually, using maxpooling
pooled_out = downsample.max_pool_2d(
    input=conv_out,
    ds=poolsize,
    ignore_border=True
)
```

When initializing the weight values, the no.of feature maps, input and the receptive field's size determine the fan-in. In closing, the Logistic Regression class that is defined in MNIST Classification digits and the Hidden Layer class that is defined in Multilayer Perception can be instantiated in the network as follows.

```python
x = T.matrix('x')    # the data is presented as rasterized images
y = T.ivector('y')   # the labels are presented as 1D vector of
                     # [int] labels

######################
# BUILD ACTUAL MODEL #
######################
print '... building the model'

# Reshape matrix of rasterized images of shape (batch_size, 28 * 28)
# to a 4D tensor, compatible with our LeNetConvPoolLayer
# (28, 28) is the size of MNIST images.
layer0_input = x.reshape((batch_size, 1, 28, 28))

# Construct the first convolutional pooling layer:
# filtering reduces the image size to (28-5+1 , 28-5+1) = (24, 24)
# maxpooling reduces this further to (24/2, 24/2) = (12, 12)
# 4D output tensor is thus of shape (batch_size, nkerns[0], 12, 12)
layer0 = LeNetConvPoolLayer(
    rng,
    input=layer0_input,
    image_shape=(batch_size, 1, 28, 28),
    filter_shape=(nkerns[0], 1, 5, 5),
    poolsize=(2, 2)
)

# Construct the second convolutional pooling layer
# filtering reduces the image size to (12-5+1, 12-5+1) = (8, 8)
# maxpooling reduces this further to (8/2, 8/2) = (4, 4)
# 4D output tensor is thus of shape (batch_size, nkerns[1], 4, 4)
layer1 = LeNetConvPoolLayer(
    rng,
    input=layer0.output,
    image_shape=(batch_size, nkerns[0], 12, 12),
    filter_shape=(nkerns[1], nkerns[0], 5, 5),
```

```python
    poolsize=(2, 2)
)

# the HiddenLayer being fully-connected, it operates on 2D matrices of
# shape (batch_size, num_pixels) (i.e matrix of rasterized images).
# This will generate a matrix of shape (batch_size, nkerns[1] * 4 * 4),
# or (500, 50 * 4 * 4) = (500, 800) with the default values.
layer2_input = layer1.output.flatten(2)

# construct a fully-connected sigmoidal layer
layer2 = HiddenLayer(
    rng,
    input=layer2_input,
    n_in=nkerns[1] * 4 * 4,
    n_out=500,
    activation=T.tanh
)

# classify the values of the fully-connected sigmoidal layer
layer3 = LogisticRegression(input=layer2.output, n_in=500, n_out=10)

# the cost we minimize during training is the NLL of the model
cost = layer3.negative_log_likelihood(y)

# create a function to compute the mistakes that are made by the model
test_model = theano.function(
    [index],
    layer3.errors(y),
    givens={
        x: test_set_x[index * batch_size: (index + 1) * batch_size],
        y: test_set_y[index * batch_size: (index + 1) * batch_size]
    }
)

validate_model = theano.function(
    [index],
    layer3.errors(y),
    givens={
        x: valid_set_x[index * batch_size: (index + 1) * batch_size],
        y: valid_set_y[index * batch_size: (index + 1) * batch_size]
    }
)

# create a list of all model parameters to be fit by gradient descent
params = layer3.params + layer2.params + layer1.params + layer0.params

# create a list of gradients for all model parameters
grads = T.grad(cost, params)

# train_model is a function that updates the model parameters by
# SGD Since this model has many parameters, it would be tedious to
# manually create an update rule for each model parameter. We thus
# create the updates list by automatically looping over all
```

```
# (params[i], grads[i]) pairs.
updates = [
    (param_i, param_i - learning_rate * grad_i)
    for param_i, grad_i in zip(params, grads)
]

train_model = theano.function(
    [index],
    cost,
    updates=updates,
    givens={
        x: train_set_x[index * batch_size: (index + 1) * batch_size],
        y: train_set_y[index * batch_size: (index + 1) * batch_size]
    }
)
```

Since the code that does all the early stopping and the training is similar to the MLP, it is left out. The code can then be called:

python code/convolutional_mlp.py

Some of the output that you should see include

```
Optimization complete.
Best validation score of 0.910000 % obtained at
iteration 17800, with test

performance 0.920000 %
The code for file convolutional_mlp.py ran for 380.28m
```

Chapter 4: Classes of Learning Algorithms

We are now going to learn about the learning algorithms like linear methods, neural networks, nearest neighbor methods and support vector machines.

Linear Methods

It is one of the oldest supervised ML algorithms in statistics. The main assumption is on the variable output Y, which is of H. The variable Y is a description of the collection of linear variables that are used as input, they are, $X_1,....X_p$ (i.e as a Hyperplane). When it comes to Regression, H includes models that are of the form:

$$\varphi(x) = b + \sum_{j=1}^{p} x_j w_j$$

When it comes to binary classification, we have y=({c1,c2}), H includes all models that are of the form:

$$\varphi(x) = \begin{cases} c_1 & \text{if } b + \sum_{j=1}^{p} x_j w_j > 0 \\ c_2 & \text{otherwise} \end{cases}$$

When you have a good separating hyperplane, it uses the distance to the training data points that are near.

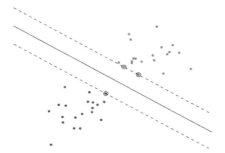

There are very many types of linear methods that differ in ways that bring about an estimation of the coefficients of b and W_j, (for j=1,...,p), it often uses specific optimization procedures that are specific to reduce the criterion. The most popular is the *least square* method. It comprises of the coefficients b and w_j which reduces the re-substitution estimate, by the use of squared error loss.

Linear methods despite their simplicity, they can provide reliable predictions and an interpretable description of how the output is affected by the input variables. Linear methods against their title can model X and Y which are nonlinear models. For instance, the application of methods used to transform variable inputs.

Support vector machines

If data points that are in a learning set are separable in a linear manner, some hyperplanes exist, which are equally good when re-substitution is evaluated. However, in generalization, the hyperplanes are usually inequivalent. As you can see in the image above, a good separation is completely achieved when the margin to the closest training data is large; when the margin is large, the model's generalization error will be low.

Support vector machine is used in max-margin linear models. If we assume that the generality loss does not exist, and we also assume that b=0 and y={-1,1}; support vector machines solve the primal optimization problem for them to be learned.

$$\min_{\mathbf{w}, \xi} \left\{ \frac{1}{2} \|\mathbf{w}\|^2 + C \sum_{i=1}^{N} \xi_i \right\}$$

Subject to $\quad y_i(\mathbf{w} \cdot \mathbf{x}_i) \geq 1 - \xi_i, \quad \xi_i \geq 0.$

The optimization problem is as below in its dual.

$$\max_{\alpha} \left\{ \sum_{i=1}^{N} \alpha_i - \frac{1}{2} \sum_{i,j} \alpha_i \alpha_j y_i y_j \mathbf{x}_i \cdot \mathbf{x}_j \right\}$$

This is now subject to $0 \leqslant \alpha_i \leqslant C$,

C here is a hyper-parameter used to control the model's misclassification degree, in case of linearly inseparable classes. Identifying with the dual problem solution, then

$$\mathbf{w} = \sum_{i=1}^{N} \alpha_i y_i x_i,$$

Where the expression of the linear model is done.

Support vector machines use an input space that is original, which is projected to a Kernel trick that is a high-dimension projection, in order to get to a classification that is nonlinear; the kernel trick is the place where the separating hyperplane can be found. You will be shocked to discover, that the problem found in the dual optimization is the same, but xi.xj, which is the dot product is not used. Instead, a replacement by kernel K(xi,xj) that corresponds the dot product x_i & x_j in the space that is new.

Neural Networks

The neural network family roots back to discover the mathematical representation of processing information in bio-matter. We know this is a far reaching objective; artificial neural networks have bridged the gap statistically, and it has grown to be one effective method in ML.

There are several units called neurons in a neural network. They exist in the form of

$$h_j(\mathbf{x}) = \sigma(w_j + \sum_{i=1}^{n} w_{ij} x_i),$$

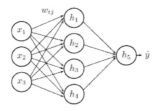

σ is an activation function that is nonlinear, just like the function of sigmoid or the activation of Softmax. In most cases, the units are laid out in successive layers, where layer inputs go towards the weighted connections which are recognized as *synapses*, to the next layer's inputs. The example on the diagram above, we are looking at a neural network that has 3 layers. The 1st layer is obviously the layer concerned with inputs which transmits the values $x=(x_1,...x_p)$ as inputs to the 2nd layer. In the 2nd layer, there are activation units $h_j$which take values of the input layer that are weighted, that produce outputs which are used in nonlinear transformations. Looking at the 3rd layer, it comprises of a one activation unit, that takes the weighted outputs of the 2nd layer as inputs, which then produce the predicted value ŷ. we assume that we have a fixed structure, and all the network units utilize the identical activation function represented as σ, then the space of H hypothesis has the models represented by φ in the form:

$$\varphi(x) = \sigma(w_5 + \sum_{j=1}^{4} w_{j5}\sigma(w_j + \sum_{i=1}^{p} w_{ij}x_i)).$$

When it comes to linear methods, there is an estimation of weights w_{ij} when it comes to learning a neural network.These weights minimize the loss function but in a specific way, using optimization procedures that are specific. Among the methods, *back propagation* algorithm is the most famous method. The most advanced level of neural networks, deep learning, has proven the potential of the models to independently learn high-level data and also the representation of efficient data. On different hard tasks, like speech recognition,the neural network have accomplished greater milestones and achievements, image classification, shining past human capabilities and other automated methods.

Theoretically, it is not known as to what makes them tick. Particularly, when it comes to selecting the right combination of units, types of activation-function and layers is still a very fragile process that makes it hard for non-experts to use neural networks.

Nearest neighbor methods

These methods are of a nonparametric algorithm class. These algorithms are known as prototype methods. These methods are different because they rely on memory and they do not need to be fit in any model. They exist based on the principle of using new samples that are discovered after finding training samples that are close to them. The new sample then infers the output variable's value. When it comes to regression, the k-nearest neighbor-algorithm makes an average of the values of the output from the k closest training-samples. I.e.

$$\varphi(\mathbf{x}) = \frac{1}{k} \sum_{(\mathbf{x}_i, y_i) \in NN(\mathbf{x}, \mathcal{L}, k)} y_i,$$

In this equation, we have NN(x, L,k) as a representation of the k nearest neighbors of x in L. Classification uses the same procedure, without using the output value that is predicted which is computed as the majority class in the k nearest neighbors:

$$\varphi(\mathbf{x}) = \arg\max_{c \in \mathcal{Y}} \sum_{(\mathbf{x}_i, y_i) \in NN(\mathbf{x}, \mathcal{L}, k)} 1(y_i = c).$$

The distant function that you might decide to use to identify the k-nearest neighbors has the possibility to be any kind of metric. One variant to take note of is the neighbor algorithm that is radius-based, where the output value that is predicted is calculated from the samples that are in training, which is in a new samples radius. In areas that have non-uniform sample data, the last algorithm can be a better alternative, compared to the method of the k-nearest neighbor.

Even though they are simple, nearest neighbor methods provide good results. They classify successfully, where there is an irregular decision boundary. Theoretically, the proof of the methods consistency is important. When the L size does not have an end, and k adjusts perfectly to L, the k-nearest neighbor generalization error production converges to the Bayes model generalization error.

Chapter 5: Classification of Regression Trees

We are going to look into detail the decision tree methods. We will provide an overview on how the algorithm has been developed. We will then present a mathematical presentation to introduce the notation and concepts. We will then present the learning algorithm.

Introduction

Artificial intelligence has been progressed by the curiosity of mankind who tries to understand and make use of complex data. This is through finding models that predict accurately and extract knowledge intelligently. This two sides realization has made strides in machine learning, giving rise to research in different fields. Tree based methods are by far one of the useful and effective methods that can produce understandable and reliable results on any data.

In 1963, decision trees appeared through the first tree called automatic - interaction detector which is used in the handling of non-addictive multivariate effects in the survey data. Improvements were placed on AID and more computer programs were proposed for exploratory advances.

Decision trees are now by the state of the art algorithms that includes forests or boosting methods. This is where they come in handy as building blocks for the building of large models. It is therefore important to understand the details of the algorithm of single decision trees, to analyze these methods.

Tree Structured Models

When we have finite values as the output space, like in classification, which has $y=\{c_1,c_2,...,c_j\}$, you can look at supervised leaning-problem, by noticing how Y makes a universal partition, in the universe Ω, I .e.

$$\Omega=\Omega_{c1}U \quad \Omega...U \quad \Omega_{cj}$$

Ω_{ck} represents the object set where Y has C_k value. The classifier ϕ similarly, can be regarded as universe Ω partition sin

$\hat{y}$ of Y. The definition of the partition is however expressed using x input space, instead of Ω. I.e.

$$\mathcal{X} = \mathcal{X}_{c_1}^{\varphi} \cup \mathcal{X}_{c_2}^{\varphi} \cup ... \cup \mathcal{X}_{c_J}^{\varphi},$$

This is where. $\mathcal{X}_{c_k}^{\varphi}$ is the description vectors set $x \in \mathcal{X}$ that ϕ (x)=C_k. Learning a partition of x that matches the best partition, becomes synonymous to learning a classifier. I.e., using the model of Bayes ϕ B over x that endangers it:

$$\mathcal{X} = \mathcal{X}_{c_1}^{\varphi_B} \cup \mathcal{X}_{c_2}^{\varphi_B} \cup ... \cup \mathcal{X}_{c_J}^{\varphi_B}.$$

Partitioning when there is noise

When you discover that X=x does not determine Y, where you have noise Y, then 2 objects that are distinct exist form the universe Ω. The rep x_1 and x_2 are equal in the input space, even though output values y1 and y2 are corresponding but different. H_t means that the subsets most probably will not disjoint.

$$\mathcal{X}_{c_L}^{\Omega} = \{x_i | i \in \Omega, Y = c_k\}$$

Generally, models that are tree structured are simple. It can approximate the model of Bayes partition by having the input space partitioned recursively. It uses subspaces to assign the prediction values that are constant to objects that are in the terminal subspace. For clarity, the following concepts need to be determined.

A graph G=(V, E) represents a tree that has one path that has 2 connections of node

A tree that is rooted is one that has been assigned to the root. An assumption can be made that a directed graph is the rooted tree where the nodes are directed far off the root.

When in a tree that is rooted, a node is described as internal if it has one, or more than one child.

A binary tree is a tree that is rooted and has two children in all its internal nodes.

A binary tree or a tree structure's description can be in the form of a model $\phi : x$ any model is the one that describes the node this a representation of an input's space subspace, where the root node t_0 corresponds to x itself.

Induction and Decision Trees

Decision tree learning leads to determining the tree structure that produces the partition closest to the engineered partition Y over X. Decision tree construction is driven by the goal of getting a model that partitions the set of learning L in detail. From all types of decision trees, several might explain L very well. If we go by the Occam's Razor principles that prefer the explanation that makes a few assumptions, that favor a simple result that is suitable for the statistics. L is understood from a decision tree by the discovery of a small tree ϕ^*, minimizing the estimates re-substitution. From a generalization perspective, this assumption is definitive regarding interoperability. A small decision tree is easy to understand than a complex-large tree.

When you are discovering the smallest-tree ϕ^* reduces the estimation from being re-replication, this is referred to as NP-complete difficulty. As a result, when we speculate that P $\neq$ NP, we are g efficient in finding ϕ^*. This suggests that the discovery of efficient heuristics that will be used in constructing near-optimal decision-trees makes it possible to have computation requirements in a realistic boundary.

For more information regarding Induction and decision trees, follow the link below

https://people.cs.umass.edu/~utgoff/papers/mlj-id5r.pdf

https://courses.cs.ut.ee/2009/bayesian-networks/extras/quinlan1986.pdf

Chapter 6: Random Forests

Bias Variance Decomposition

The error of model ϕ_L generalization is the anticipated error of prediction when you look at the loss function L

$Err(\phi_L)=E_{XY}\{L(Y,\phi_L(x))\}$

The expected error of prediction of ϕ_L at X=x can be expressed as

$Err(\varphi_L(x)) = \mathbb{E}_{Y|X=x}\{L(Y, \varphi_L(x))\}.$

When you look at regression, the loss of error squared, the result of error predicted is the anticipated disintegration of variance, a bias that comprises a useful framework for diagnosing the model's prediction error. When you get into the classifications zero-one, it is hard to obtain the same decomposition. The variance and bias concepts transpose in different ways into classification, providing frameworks that are comparable to the study of prediction classifiers error.

Regression

When you look at regression, and you assume L as the squared error loss, the model of prediction error ϕ_L at point X=x can be rephrased according to Bayes model ϕ_B:

$Err(\varphi_L(x))$

$= \mathbb{E}_{Y|X=x}\{(Y - \varphi_L(x))^2\}$
$= \mathbb{E}_{Y|X=x}\{(Y - \varphi_B(x) + \varphi_B(x) - \varphi_L(x))^2\}$
$= \mathbb{E}_{Y|X=x}\{(Y - \varphi_B(x))^2\} + \mathbb{E}_{Y|X=x}\{(\varphi_B(x) - \varphi_L(x))^2\}$
$\hookrightarrow + \mathbb{E}_{Y|X=x}\{2(Y - \varphi_B(x))(\varphi_B(x) - \varphi_L(x))\}$
$= \mathbb{E}_{Y|X=x}\{(Y - \varphi_B(x))^2\} + \mathbb{E}_{Y|X=x}\{(\varphi_B(x) - \varphi_L(x))^2\}$
$= Err(\varphi_B(x)) + \{\varphi_B(x) - \varphi_L(x)\}^2$

By Bayes model regression, $\mathbb{E}_{Y|X=x}\{Y - \varphi_B(x)\} = \mathbb{E}_{Y|X=x}\{Y\} - \varphi_B(x) = 0$. The last expression in the equation tallies with the irreducible error at X=x the 2nd term in the variation of ϕ_L taken from Bayes model. If the distance is greater from the Bayes model. The error enlarges as the sub-suitable model grows enormous.

If there is an assumption that the learning set L is a random variable and there is a deterministic learning algorithm, inconsistencies with L in the Bayes model is articulated in projecting $E_L\{\phi_L(\mathbf{x})\}$ above the proficient models by understanding the feasible sets of N:

$$\mathbb{E}_{\mathcal{L}}\{(\varphi_B(\mathbf{x}) - \varphi_{\mathcal{L}}(\mathbf{x}))^2\}$$
$$= \mathbb{E}_{\mathcal{L}}\{(\varphi_B(\mathbf{x}) - \mathbb{E}_{\mathcal{L}}\{\varphi_{\mathcal{L}}(\mathbf{x})\} + \mathbb{E}_{\mathcal{L}}\{\varphi_{\mathcal{L}}(\mathbf{x})\} - \varphi_{\mathcal{L}}(\mathbf{x}))^2\}$$
$$= \mathbb{E}_{\mathcal{L}}\{(\varphi_B(\mathbf{x}) - \mathbb{E}_{\mathcal{L}}\{\varphi_{\mathcal{L}}(\mathbf{x})\})^2\} + \mathbb{E}_{\mathcal{L}}\{(\mathbb{E}_{\mathcal{L}}\{\varphi_{\mathcal{L}}(\mathbf{x})\} - \varphi_{\mathcal{L}}(\mathbf{x}))^2\}$$
$$\hookrightarrow + \mathbb{E}_{\mathcal{L}}\{2(\varphi_B(\mathbf{x}) - \mathbb{E}_{\mathcal{L}}\{\varphi_{\mathcal{L}}(\mathbf{x})\})(\mathbb{E}_{\mathcal{L}}\{\varphi_{\mathcal{L}}(\mathbf{x})\} - \varphi_{\mathcal{L}}(\mathbf{x}))\}$$
$$= \mathbb{E}_{\mathcal{L}}\{(\varphi_B(\mathbf{x}) - \mathbb{E}_{\mathcal{L}}\{\varphi_{\mathcal{L}}(\mathbf{x})\})^2\} + \mathbb{E}_{\mathcal{L}}\{(\mathbb{E}_{\mathcal{L}}\{\varphi_{\mathcal{L}}(\mathbf{x})\} - \varphi_{\mathcal{L}}(\mathbf{x}))^2\}$$
$$= (\varphi_B(\mathbf{x}) - \mathbb{E}_{\mathcal{L}}\{\varphi_{\mathcal{L}}(\mathbf{x})\})^2 + \mathbb{E}_{\mathcal{L}}\{(\mathbb{E}_{\mathcal{L}}\{\varphi_{\mathcal{L}}(\mathbf{x})\} - \varphi_{\mathcal{L}}(\mathbf{x}))^2\} \quad (4.4)$$

Since $\mathbb{E}_{\mathcal{L}}\{\mathbb{E}_{\mathcal{L}}\{\varphi_{\mathcal{L}}(\mathbf{x})\} - \varphi_{\mathcal{L}}(\mathbf{x})\} = \mathbb{E}_{\mathcal{L}}\{\varphi_{\mathcal{L}}(\mathbf{x})\} - \mathbb{E}_{\mathcal{L}}\{\varphi_{\mathcal{L}}(\mathbf{x})\} = 0.$ in conclusion, the generalization error expected decomposes additively in the theory below.

Theorem

Bias variance decomposition is from loss error squared; the anticipated generalization error $\mathbb{E}_{\mathcal{L}}\{\text{Err}\{\varphi_{\mathcal{L}}(\mathbf{x})\}\}$ at $X = \mathbf{x}$ is

$$\mathbb{E}_{\mathcal{L}}\{\text{Err}(\varphi_{\mathcal{L}}(\mathbf{x}))\} = noise(\mathbf{x}) + bias^2(\mathbf{x}) + var(\mathbf{x}),$$

where

$$noise(\mathbf{x}) = \text{Err}(\varphi_B(\mathbf{x})),$$
$$bias^2(\mathbf{x}) = (\varphi_B(\mathbf{x}) - \mathbb{E}_{\mathcal{L}}\{\varphi_{\mathcal{L}}(\mathbf{x})\})^2,$$
$$var(\mathbf{x}) = \mathbb{E}_{\mathcal{L}}\{(\mathbb{E}_{\mathcal{L}}\{\varphi_{\mathcal{L}}(\mathbf{x})\} - \varphi_{\mathcal{L}}(\mathbf{x}))^2\}.$$

This bias-variance-decomposition of the error of generalization was discussed in neural networks in 1992. The idiom $noise(\mathbf{x})$ is a lingering error. The algorithm is free of the learning set. It also provides a theoretical lower bound on the generalization error. $Bias^2$ makes a measure of the discrepancy between the Bayes model projection and an average projection. $var(\mathbf{x})$ Computes other variabilities of the X=x variations over the models.

Chapter 7: How to Interpret Random Forests

A response variable prediction based on prediction variables that are set is an important expedition in science. The aim is to make accurate response prediction; but to accurately single out predictor variables crucial in creating projections, like, for instance, is to understand the underlying process. Since they are used in many problem scenarios, and their accuracy to build models that are accurate, and in the provision of the importance measures, the major data analysis tool that I used successfully, in different scenarios is the random forests.

Despite the wide applications, there are only a few works that have looked into the algorithms theoretical and statistical mechanisms and properties.

Variable importance

When you factor in single-decision trees, the measure of importance of the variables Xj was as

$$\text{Imp}(X_j) = \sum_{t \in \varphi} \Delta I(\tilde{s}_t^j, t),$$

Where $\tilde{s}_t^j$ is the understudy split for s_t, which is a split closely defined on variable X_j that mirrors the split s_t interpreted in t node. Surrogate splits were used to account for masking-effects. However, if X_{j2} another tree is grown in place of the removal of X_{j1}, then the second split may occur in the tree and split with the results may relatively be as great as the first tree. When this happens, then the relevant measure detects the X_{j2} importance.

Asymptotic analysis

A tree that is totally random and developed is a decision tree with t node being separated by the use of a variable X_j that was selected in a consistent erratic manner among the neglected parent-nodes t, that split to [Xj] sub trees.

In these trees, the depth is similar to all leaves$_p$ and those at st of grown tree is bijection with X of the feasible joint configuration of a variable. An instance is, all variable inputs are in binary, the forthcoming of the tree will have 2^p leaves.

Non-totally randomized trees

Built at random, the trees are not related to those extremely randomized trees or random forests. To comprehend the algorithms that are computed, take an alternative of node t of randomized trees, drawn equally at random $1 \leq K \leq p$ variables. Choose one that utilizes $\Delta i(t)$. Like previously, t is split to several sub-trees like the cardinality of the variable that is chosen. Know that, K=1, it aggregates to the construction of classical trees that are single in a way that is deterministic.

Chapter 8: Ensemble of Random Patches

The algorithm of random patches that is being proposed is a method that can be looked at in the following way. If you have $\mathcal{R}(\alpha_s, \alpha_f, \mathcal{L})$, that is an all random set of $\alpha_s N \times \alpha_f P$ size, which the L database is obtained from, N enumerates to the samples of L which is its input variables and $\alpha_s \in [0, 1]$ is a hyper-parameter that has control over the samples found in a patch; this shows that $\mathcal{R}(\alpha_s, \alpha_f, \mathcal{L})$ represents a set of subsets that contain $\alpha_s N$ samples that have $\alpha_f P$ variables. Below is how the method can be described.

Algorithm of Random Patches

```
1: for m = 1,..., M do
2:     Draw a patch r ~ U(R(αs, αf, L)) uniformly at random
3:     Build a model on the selected patch r
4: end for
5: Aggregate the predictions of the M models in an ensemble
```

Different base estimators can be exploited using the RP algorithm, but we are only going to consider estimators that are tree-based. RP algorithm is evaluated by the use of classification trees that are standard, as well as randomized trees that are extreme. If there is no explicit statement on the trees, the Gini index is used to grow and prune the trees as a criterion for the splitting node. The randomized trees that are extreme have parameter K, which is a set in RP of a maximum value $K = \alpha_f P$. This set does not correspond to other variables that are randomly selected.

One benefit of Random Patches is that it makes a generalization of Pasting Rvotes together with the algorithm of Random Subspace. Both of these cases are cases of the setting of RP $\alpha_s = 1.0$ which yields RS, as set $\alpha_f = 1.0$ produces P. When hyper-parameters α_s and α_f are simultaneously turned, RP is expected to be as good as the methods seen. The only requirement is that in the tuning instance, over-fitting is not allowed.

Level decision trees that have base estimators, there are parallels that can be derived from RF and RP algorithms. For $\alpha_s = 1.0$ value of $\alpha_f P$ is almost equal to K feature numbers that are assessed node splitting occurs. There is a difference that still exists. Subsets features in RP are globally selected at once, before a tree construction. On the contrary, RF subset features are derived from each local node. It is clear that the RP approach can be used easily when one is working with huge databases. One does not need to consider features that are not selected.This now lowers the memory needs that are needed when a tree is being built. One other interesting parallel happens when there is the use of bootstrap samples, like how it is used in RF. A set $\alpha_b = 0.632,$ is normally close. This is an indication of the proportion averaging of samples that are unique in a sample bootstrap. The differences that exist are such that, in bootstrap samples, the unique samples that are being trained vary, compared to RP that has fixed 0.632N. The other difference is in the unequal weights of the samples in bootstrap.

Additionally, RP is related to the algorithms referred to as SubBag, which is known to combine RS and Bagging for the ensembles construction. When samples of N boot-strapped that were almost equal to $\alpha_b = 0.632$ and $\alpha_f = 0.75,$ it was proposed that the performance of SubBag is much more, compared to RF's performance. One RF's advantage is that it applies to any base estimator.

Accuracy Needs

The validation we have seen of RP algorithm is done in 2steps. We need to first look at how RP stacks to other ensemble methods that are tree based, in the context of accuracy. We then need to look at its memory requirements in order to achieve accuracy and also to determine the capability of the algorithm to take charge of memory constraints that are strong; this is also compared to alternative ensemble methods.

When you are looking at accuracy α_b and α_f give off degrees of freedom that are considered. It is to remarkably improve or reduce RP's performance. On a first impression basis, it is possible for one to presume that due to base estimators being built on parts of data, the ensembles accuracy will be low if you compare it with the whole set used to construct the base estimators. Our aim is to see if the features that are being sampled globally, lower their performance, compared to local sampling. This is now the main difference between the more modern RF, and the more old school RP.

Protocol

Comparison of our method is done with RS, RF, and P. 2 variant considerations have been considered for P, RS, and RP. One variant uses decision trees that are standard, as base estimators, while the other uses base estimators of randomized trees that are extreme. In general, the comparison takes place in 8 methods. RP-DT, P-ET, P-DT, RS-ET, RF, ET, RS-DT, and RP-ET.

The method's accuracy is calculated using a list that is extensive, which has both classification and artificial problems. 3 random partitions exist in every data set: the 1st and bigger half of the actual data set is for training: 2nd 25% is for validation and the last 25% is for testing. Hyper-parameters α_s and α_r in all methods were tuned with grid-search procedures on the set of validation. The grid that was used was {0.01, 0.1..., 0.9, 1.0} for α_s and α_r. Default values were given to the other hyper-parameters. In ET and RF, the selected features of K are chosen at random at each node, tuned by the use of α_{rp} grid. If one was to look at all the ensembles, two hundred and fifty trees that flourished were produced; with a generalization of the estimated set of testing. The procedure repetition was done 50 times, for all methods and data sets. This was done by the use of the fifty random partitions that were used in the methods.

Data sets that are small

We need to try out our approach on the data sets that are small, before going into heavy experimentation. To achieve this, experiments have been carried out on sixteen public data sets that will be seen in *Table 1* below, which was found in a repository of a machine learning in UCI. The data sets obtained cover a number of conditions, as well as the range of sample sizes, that start from 208 and end up at 20000, and the variable features range from 6 up to 168. *Table 2* below has a detailed performance of the eight methods for all sixteen data sets, with the help of the protocol that has been discussed above. We are going to make an analysis of the trends by conducting several tests of statistics.

First, we performed the Friedman test rebating the theory detailing the equality of each and every algorithm at a crucial level $\alpha = 0.05$. Then we did the Nemenyi test, to compare the pairwise of the eight-methods average ranking. This test showed that 2 classifiers are different (at $\alpha = 0.05$), if there is a difference in their ranking average, by at minimum the critical difference = 2.6249.

Table 1

Dataset	N	p
DIABETES	768	8
DIG44	18000	16
IONOSPHERE	351	34
PENDIGITS	10992	16
LETTER	20000	16
LIVER	345	6
MUSK2	6598	168
RING-NORM	10000	20
SATELLITE	6435	36
SEGMENT	2310	19
SONAR	208	60
STAMBASE	4601	57
TWO-NORM	9999	20
VEHICLE	1692	18
VOWEL	990	10
WAVEFORM	5000	21

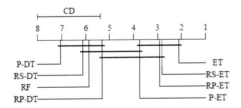

Figure1: Average ranking of small data sets and methods

Figure 1 makes a summary of the comparisons. The line at the top is the axis where the average tank R_m is plotted in each model, from the worst methods (highest rank) that are on the left side, to the best method (lowest rank) that is on the right. Statistically, similar method groups are connected together. Critical Difference is well exhibited in the diagram above. To support the ranking comparisons we have looked at, a 50 accuracy comparison is done over each split of data set for each method, by the use of a paired t-test (with $\alpha = 0.01$). The comparison results are then summarized in the table below in the context of 'Win-Draw-Loss' method pair statuses. When you see the intersection of 3 values of column j and row i, it shows the number of data set methods i is not different than j method.

Validation	RF	ET	P-DT	P-ET	RS-DT	RS-ET	RP-DT	RP-ET
DIABETES	77.12 (6)	77.25 (5)	77.67 (4)	78.01 (3)	75.11 (8)	76.77 (7)	78.82 (2)	79.07 (1)
DJG44	94.99 (7)	95.78 (1)	91.86 (8)	95.46 (4)	95.07 (6)	95.69 (3)	95.13 (5)	95.72 (2)
IONOSPHERE	94.40 (6)	95.15 (3)	93.86 (8)	94.75 (5)	94.11 (7)	94.90 (4)	95.20 (2)	95.36 (1)
PENDIGITS	98.94 (7)	99.33 (1)	98.09 (8)	99.28 (4)	99.02 (6)	99.31 (3)	99.07 (5)	99.32 (2)
LETTER	95.36 (7)	96.38 (1)	92.72 (8)	95.87 (4)	95.68 (6)	96.08 (3)	95.74 (5)	96.10 (2)
LIVER	72.37 (5)	71.90 (6)	72.55 (4)	72.88 (3)	68.06 (8)	70.88 (7)	74.53 (1)	74.37 (2)
MUSK2	97.18 (7)	97.73 (1)	96.89 (8)	97.60 (4)	97.58 (6)	97.72 (3)	97.60 (5)	97.73 (2)
RING-NORM	97.44 (6)	98.10 (5)	96.41 (8)	97.28 (7)	98.25 (4)	98.41 (3)	98.50 (2)	98.54 (1)
SATELLITE	90.97 (7)	91.56 (1)	90.01 (8)	91.40 (5)	91.31 (6)	91.50 (3)	91.41 (4)	91.54 (2)
SEGMENT	97.46 (6)	98.17 (2)	96.78 (8)	98.10 (4)	97.33 (7)	98.14 (3)	97.52 (5)	98.21 (1)
SONAR	82.92 (7)	86.92 (3)	80.03 (8)	84.73 (5)	83.07 (6)	87.07 (2)	85.42 (4)	88.15 (1)
SPAMBASE	94.80 (7)	95.36 (3)	93.69 (8)	95.01 (6)	95.01 (5)	95.50 (2)	95.11 (4)	95.57 (1)
TWO-NORM	97.54 (6)	97.77 (2)	97.52 (7)	97.59 (5)	97.46 (8)	97.63 (4)	97.76 (3)	97.82 (1)
VEHICLE	88.67 (5)	88.68 (4)	88.26 (8)	88.74 (3)	88.41 (7)	88.60 (6)	89.22 (1)	89.21 (2)
VOWEL	92.04 (5)	95.12 (1)	85.19 (8)	93.49 (4)	89.76 (7)	94.34 (3)	91.10 (6)	94.48 (2)
WAVEFORM	85.45 (6)	85.96 (2)	84.89 (8)	85.68 (5)	84.91 (7)	85.69 (4)	85.85 (3)	86.21 (1)
Average rank	6.25	2.5625	7.4375	4.4375	6.5	3.75	3.5626	1.5

Test	RF	ET	P-DT	P-ET	RS-DT	RS-ET	RP-DT	RP-ET
DIABETES	75.62 (4)	75.38 (5)	75.67 (3)	76.34 (1)	73.03 (8)	74.63 (7)	75.32 (6)	75.82 (2)
DJG44	94.96 (6)	95.67 (1)	91.79 (8)	95.39 (4)	94.98 (5)	95.58 (2)	94.95 (7)	95.55 (3)
IONOSPHERE	92.20 (6)	93.22 (1)	92.09 (7)	92.40 (4)	92.02 (8)	93.22 (2)	92.34 (5)	92.68 (3)
PENDIGITS	98.84 (7)	99.23 (1)	97.97 (8)	99.21 (3)	98.95 (5)	99.21 (2)	98.93 (6)	99.20 (4)
LETTER	95.27 (7)	96.29 (1)	92.57 (8)	95.89 (4)	95.61 (5)	96.03 (2)	95.61 (6)	95.99 (3)
LIVER	69.53 (3)	68.22 (6)	70.43 (1)	69.58 (5)	63.17 (8)	67.35 (7)	70.20 (2)	69.67 (4)
MUSK2	97.08 (7)	97.61 (1)	96.69 (8)	97.54 (4)	97.47 (5)	97.58 (2)	97.42 (6)	97.56 (3)
RING-NORM	97.48 (6)	98.07 (5)	96.42 (8)	97.25 (7)	98.16 (4)	98.31 (1)	98.22 (3)	98.30 (2)
SATELLITE	90.67 (7)	91.22 (2)	89.66 (8)	91.20 (3)	91.15 (5)	91.28 (1)	91.04 (6)	91.20 (4)
SEGMENT	97.02 (5)	97.93 (1)	96.44 (8)	97.86 (3)	96.86 (7)	97.90 (2)	96.88 (6)	97.84 (4)
SONAR	79.53 (5)	82.76 (1)	75.15 (8)	80.07 (4)	78.50 (6)	82.19 (2)	78.26 (7)	81.92 (3)
SPAMBASE	94.76 (7)	95.17 (3)	93.51 (8)	94.84 (5)	94.88 (4)	95.22 (2)	94.80 (6)	95.22 (1)
TWO-NORM	97.22 (7)	97.50 (1)	97.26 (6)	97.29 (4)	97.20 (8)	97.33 (2)	97.33 (3)	97.28 (5)
VEHICLE	87.47 (7)	87.85 (3)	87.01 (8)	87.98 (2)	87.50 (6)	87.68 (5)	87.73 (4)	88.08 (1)
VOWEL	91.51 (5)	93.95 (1)	84.17 (8)	92.93 (4)	89.51 (7)	93.60 (2)	89.89 (6)	93.09 (3)
WAVEFORM	85.23 (5)	85.77 (1)	84.68 (8)	85.40 (3)	84.74 (7)	85.38 (4)	85.16 (6)	85.56 (2)
Average rank	5.875	2.125	7.0625	3.75	6.125	2.8125	5.3125	2.9375

Table 2: Percentage accuracy on small data sets

	RF	ET	P-DT	P-ET	RS-DT	RS-ET	RP-DT	RP-ET
RF	—	1/2/13	12/4/0	1/7/8	4/7/5	2/2/12	1/10/5	0/4/12
ET	13/2/1	—	14/1/1	10/5/1	13/3/0	4/11/1	12/2/2	5/10/1
P-DT	0/4/12	1/1/14	—	0/4/12	2/3/11	2/1/13	0/4/12	0/4/12
P-ET	8/7/1	1/5/10	12/4/0	—	9/6/1	2/6/8	9/6/1	0/11/5
RS-DT	5/7/4	0/3/13	11/3/2	1/6/9	—	0/2/14	1/11/4	0/4/12
RS-ET	12/2/2	1/11/4	13/1/2	8/6/2	14/2/0	—	11/4/1	1/13/2
RP-DT	5/10/1	2/2/12	12/4/0	1/6/9	4/11/1	1/4/11	—	0/6/10
RP-ET	12/4/0	1/10/5	12/4/0	5/11/0	12/4/0	2/13/1	10/6/0	—

Table 3: Pairwise t-tests comparison on small data sets

Average accuracies are not different between methods. Even though this is the case, there is some noticeable trend that appears when one is looking at *Table 1* and *Table 3*. First, ET techniques are first positioned, then DT methods that include RF algorithm. Generally, the RT algorithm comes first in ranking $R_{ET}=2.125$, and RP-ET and RS-ET follow closely at positions $R_{RP-ET}=2.9375$ and $R_{RS-ET}=2.8125$ while trailing behind, we have P-ET, $R_{P-ET}=3.75$. When you look at *Table 1*, it is ET that is ranked higher than the other DT methods. But when you look at the ET variant that is worse, P-ET maintains at nine times on a better level and one time worse than RP-DT, which is the best variant of DT. The disparity between these algorithms now becomes evident. It is now clear that when you use split thresholds that are random, instead of decision trees that are examples of optimized ones, then it pays off in the generalization context.

When you look at ET methods, RP-ET is favored to P-ET, though it is not as good as RS-ET and ET in average ranking. Because RS-ET is an RP-ET case, it is recommended that there is over-fitting when the additional parameter α_s is being tuned. RP-ET is indeed ranked better, compared to RS-ET on the validation set. *Table 3* shows otherwise and, it shows that RP-ET is better compared to RS-ET(2/13/1). When you look at ET instead of RP-ET, the performance of ET (5/10/1) is solely because subsets of ET features are re-derived locally on every node during tree construction, and not a one size fits all before the tree construction. This leads to a lower chance of generation of trees that are improper, because of initial features that are bad, leading to a better accuracy and a lower bias.

When you look at DT methods, RP-DT is first, with a mean of 5.3125, followed by RF(R_{RF}=5.875), then RS-DT R_{RS-DT}=6.125 finally AT P-DT, which is R_{P-DT}=7.0625.

Data sets that are larger

The experiments we have seen above yield some potential results, it is then fair to see if it is possible to see conclusions and generalizations on larger problems, for instance, when you are exposed to features that are hidden in thousands or genomic or non-important data. You can also try to see if it is possible to deal with features that are correlated, like images. To look into this, a 2nd experiment was conducted on thirteen large data sets, in *Table 4*. *Madelon* is the only data that is not real. When you look at the dimensions, the data sets are big and they get to thousands of samples and quite a number of features. This means that the complexity of the problem is expected to be bigger. The same protocol that was used in smaller data sets was used here. Now, to make sure that the computing times were lower on data sets that had a mark *, the methods were parsed using a hundred trees instead of two hundred and fifty, with the minimum no.of samples needed in each internal model set to 10, to manage complexity. The results are as seen in *Table 5*, and a summary of *Table 2* and *Table 6*. This is in relation to the average rank, with a critical difference at $\alpha = 0.05$, and Win/DRAW/Loss that have paired test.

After looking at *Figure 1*, it is clear that the average ranks are closer to the other in the experiment seen above. In this experiment, they are ranging from 2.38 to 6.61, while in the previous experiment, it ranges from 2.12 - 7. There is more connection with methods using critical-difference-bars. This shows how similar they are than before.

Chapter 9: Introduction of Decision Trees

Learning decision trees is an inductive reference that uses experiential techniques. The approximated detached value function that makes the data reliable and it is possible for one to learn expressions that are disjunctive.

The learning of Decision trees can approximate target functions that are discrete-valued. Learning trees can be re-represented and the readability upgraded. This is a famous inductive inference algorithm that has been applied successfully to various tasks from learning the diagnosis of medical issues to learning the access loan application risk when done on credit.

Representation of Decision tree

They are classified by decision trees that group them from starting of the tree which is the root to the leaf node. This provides a categorization of the instances. Tree nodes are a specialty in instances' experiment, with branches falling from the node to be in tune with a workable attribute value.

An example is a classification beginning at the nodes of the root of the tree; giving the specified attribute at the node a chance, descending the branch of the tree that tallies with the value of the attribute. The node has a rooted sub-tree where the procedure is repeated, that is new.

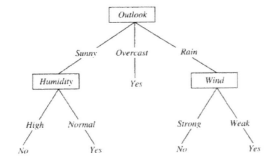

The decision tree placed above it a tennis playing concept.

In the figure above, we can see is a decision tree that is learned, and it is used to classify Saturday mornings depending on the wealth that is convenient for tennis ball playing. For instance

(Wind=Strong, Temperature=Hot, Outlook=Sunny, Humidity=High)

This can be sorted out down in the left part of the decision tree's branch that is above, the chance of it to be considered an instance would be regarded as an instance that is negative. That is, there is a tree prediction that says playing tennis is a no. Generally, there is a representation of decision trees of conjunctions and disjunction of limitations on the occurrences' trait esteems. Every way begins from the tree base of a leaf to relating to characteristic tests conjunction, and the tree setting off to a disjunction of the conjunctions. For example, the tree in the diagram above goes along with the expression

$(Outlook = Sunny \land Humidity = Normal)$

$\lor \quad (Outlook = Overcast)$

$\lor \quad (Outlook = Rain \land Wind = Weak)$

Problems that are appropriate for decision-tree learning

There are multiple selection-tree studying strategies which might be created with differing necessities and skills.Decision-tree getting to know is usually applicable flawlessly to issues with the characteristics:

The target function contains output values that are discrete

The decision-tree we have seen assigns boolean classifications, for instance, a no or a yes for the particular instance. Decision-tree techniques reach to functions of learning functions having more than 2 output values. Learning target functions are allowed by a more stable extension that has actual-valued outputs, even though the decision-tree utility is not common.

Instances are represented by attribute-value pairs.

A fixed group of attributes describes an instance; we have 'hot' values for 'Temperature'. Decision tree learning can be accredited to every attribute considered by some disjointed values, for instance, mild, cold and hot.

However, the extension allows for the algorithm to be managed with actual valued attributes, like Temperature.

Disjunctive descriptions can be a necessity. Decision trees commonly are a representation of expressions that are disjunctive.

Errors may be present in the training data. Decision-tree studying techniques might have huge errors, training instances that are in the classification errors and also in attributed values which instances are defined.

Study data with attribute values missing. Decision tree practice used when some illustrations of training having figures that are unknown. For instance, if the day's humidity is known for some training examples only.

Lots of practical problems have been discovered to fit this characteristic. Problems have been exposed to decision-tree learning like the classification of patients by the disease they are suffering from, the cause of malfunctions of the equipment, the likelihood of loan applicants depending on their repayment rate. These problems, where the task is the classification that looks at a particular set of categories, is what is known as *categorization problems.*

Decision tree studying basic algorithm

Many algorithms available are for decision-tree learning for a variation of the algorithm which is considered to the core, which employs a search that is top-down through possible decision-tree space. The approach we have seen is present in the ID3 algorithm which has a successor. This now forms a discussion.

The ID3 algorithms, using a top-down construction approach, learn the decision trees by starting with the question "what should be tested as the root of the tree? What is to be tested as the tree's root?" Every attribute instance is analyzed by an experiment that is statistical, used to determine how classification is well done in the studying examples. The applied attribute is chosen to be utilized to test the node in the root of the tree. The establishment of the node at the root's successor is done and made accessible to every attribute's value possibility, and studying samples distributed to the respective node descendant. The whole procedure is then started all over again with examples that are associated with the descendant in each node, to select the attribute that can be tested at each tree's point.

Space search Hypothesis in learning decision trees

Just like the other inductive methods of learning, ID3 can be looked at having a characteristic of space searching of a hypothesis that trains instances. The ID3 space searched hypothesis is done by some potential decision trees. ID3 does an increasing difficulty, hill-climbing hunt through the present theorem, to begin with, is an empty tree, and going ahead to consider growing hypothesis that is elaborated in the discovery of a decision that can classify training data correctly. The function of evaluation that helps in the hill-climbing is the gain measure of the information. This has been depicted in the figure below.

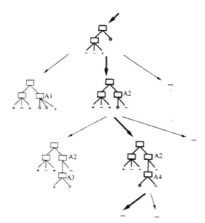

This diagram contains ID3 space search. ID3 looks for potential decision-trees in the space, from the simple to the more advanced guide by the use of the information heuristic.

When you view ID3 regarding its search strategy & search space, insight can be derived from its capabilities and disadvantages.

The hypothesis that is found in ID3 of decision trees is a dedicated area of endless discrete-valued purpose, corresponding to attributes that are available. As every limited discrete-valued task is likely to be represented by a couple of decision tree, ID3 evades some big risk of methods that search hypothesis that is incomplete.

ID3 has one present thesis going through the area of decision trees. It is collateral, an instance is the means of eliminating candidates, it is an earlier space version, it sticks with the story that the set of the constituent hypothesis has the training examples that are available. In the determination of 1 hypothesis, ID3 sheds off the capacities that allow in the explicit representation of all the hypothesis. For example, no ability to stand to determine the decision trees that are alternative and steady with the studying data that is provided.

Inductive bias in the learning of decision trees

What policy does ID3 generalize from training examples that have been observed to classify instances that are unseen? What question it began is that what is the inductive bias?When you have training examples that are collected, there are decision trees that mesh well with the examples. Describing the inductive ID3 bias points to the rationale in which selection is done in relation to theories placed. They have to reoccur more frequently than others. Which ID3 is selected by the decision-trees? The 1st tree that is acceptable is selected, and it communicates within its increasing in difficulty-hill-climbing exploration, to go through the ideal trees' space. Logically, the combing through a strategy of the ID3.

Insights on Random Forests

We are going to look at the importance of variables which are calculated from random forests. We will look at the importance of redundant variables, then we look at importance of variables when you are working with ordered variables and decision trees that are binary. Using this structure, we will look at the different sources of the bias that may happen concurrently in the computation of importance from random forests. Let us dive into the mathematics behind importance and random forests.

Inessential Variables

In most cases, the input variables in machine learning issues are parallel to each other. They also share a little bit of mutual information. This can be explained with image classification; the pixels are individual, yet they are highly parallel and individually do give or have similar information as those of their neighbors. With this in mind, variables can be partially parallel, that is, they might share some information with each other on the variable output Y.

In the extreme, unnecessariness is either complete or total. As some variables may show some excess and similar data variable output Y. To help us understand this, let's look at an example of variable inputs and the effect adding redundant variables has on randomized trees.

Two variables X_i and X_j are not required if only one can explain the other and likewise. To define redundancy:

If no additional data is needed to describe the two variables, then they are considered redundant. This means, if:

$$H(X_i|X_j) = H(X_j|X_i) = 0.$$

This is expressed if X_j and its duplicate X'_j are extremely inessential. Concerning random forests, replicates of variables if added, the split selection would not be affected. Irrespective of some redundant variables split is chosen the same, always. It does not matter if the division will be replicated severally.

Basing any of the structure generated decision trees is as a result of having a simultaneous decline in the probability of the variables being selected. Duplicated variable's nature has a huge impact on accuracy's effect. X_j has more data about the input, the splits being favored on this variable through copies being added, can lead to increase in efficiency. Over-fitting may be a result of additional copies being introduced if X_j is unrelated.

On the subject of variable importance, effects of redundant variables being added can be obtained

Quantitatively as well as qualitatively. Copies of relevant variables being added affect the importance of the replicated variable; additionally the significance of the variables is left.

Let us presume that $V = \{X_1, ..., X_p\}$ set of input variables and output Y, are computed from developed and randomized trees that are built on an enormous limitless data set. It'll be for conditioning set B:

$$I(X_i; Y|B, X_j) = I(X_j; Y|B, X_i) = 0$$
$$I(X_i; Y|B) = I(X_j; Y|B).$$

The data symmetry will be

$$I(X_i; X_j) = H(X_i) - H(X_i|X_j)$$
$$= H(X_j) - H(X_j|X_i).$$

With $H(X_i) = H(X_j)$ as $H(X_i|X_j) = H(X_i|X_j) = 0$ if the variables are redundant. As $0 \leq X_j|B$ $\leq X_j|B$ and $H(X_i|X_j) = 0$. There also $H(X_i|X_j, B) = 0$. When the argument is repeated for $I(X_i;X_j|B)$ in preference to $I(X_i;X_j)$.

Equality, in this case, carries onto any B set conditioned. As $H(X_i|B) = H(X_j|B)$ and from here, it will go on to:

$$I(X_i; Y|B, X_j) = H(X_i|B, X_j) - H(X_i|B, X_j, Y) = 0 - 0,$$
$$I(X_j; Y|B, X_i) = H(X_j|B, X_i) - H(X_j|B, X_i, Y) = 0 - 0,$$

And it can proceed to

$$I(X_i; Y|B) = H(X_i|B) - H(X_i|B, Y)$$
$$= H(X_j|B) - H(X_j|B, Y)$$
$$= I(X_j; Y|B),$$

Several propositions can be used here for instance: Proposition 1: If $X_j \in V$ is a relevant variable in connection with Y and V. If $X'_j \notin V$ is an incredibly redundant variable respecting X_j. Sample size of X_j computed with endless ensemble of totally randomized and developed random trees built $V \cup X'_j\}$ is

$$
\begin{aligned}
Imp(X_j) &= \sum_{k=0}^{p-1+1} \frac{1}{C_{p-1}^{k}} \frac{1}{p+1-k} \sum_{B \in \mathcal{P}_k(V^{-j} \cup \{X'_j\})} I(X_j; Y|B) \\
&= \sum_{k=0}^{p-1} \frac{1}{C_{p+1}^{k}} \frac{1}{p+1-k} \sum_{B \in \mathcal{P}_k(V^{-j})} I(X_j; Y|B) \\
&= \sum_{k=0}^{p-1} \frac{p-k}{p+1} \frac{1}{C_p^k} \frac{1}{p-k} \sum_{B \in \mathcal{P}_k(V^{-j})} I(X_j; Y|B),
\end{aligned}
$$

The importance of X_j decreased when X'_j, a redundant variable is added to input variables as a factor $\frac{p-k}{p+1} < 1$ replicates all information terms. Inherently, the result is anticipated since data is similar and is relayed within the confines of the two variables, that is, X_j and X'_j, its duplicate. The terms of importance are not entirely amended similarly. The weight of small conditioning sets is unchanged as those of terms with p being the large number and k representing small numbers; p-k/p+1 tends to be close to 1. While large conditioning sets have the likelihood of their weight being affected; that is large values of p-k/p+1 is 0.

Another proposition would be: Endless sample size $X_l \in V^{-j}$ is evaluated with infinite ensemble of randomized trees that are built on $V \cup \{X'_j\}$ as

$$
\begin{aligned}
Imp(X_l) &= \sum_{k=0}^{p-2} \frac{p-k}{p+1} \frac{1}{C_p^k} \frac{1}{p-k} \sum_{B \in \mathcal{P}_k(V^{-l} \setminus X_j)} I(X_l; Y|B) + \qquad (7.16) \\
&\hookrightarrow \sum_{k=0}^{p-2} \left[\sum_{k'=1}^{2} \frac{C_2^{k'}}{C_{p+1}^{k+k'}} \frac{1}{p+1-(k+k')} \right] \sum_{B \in \mathcal{P}_k(V^{-l} \setminus X_j)} I(X_l; Y|B \cup X_j).
\end{aligned}
$$

Effects of adding X_j, which is a redundant variable, and its importance on other variables X_l as $l \neq j$, is twofold.

In general, it is best if caution is applied when dealing with the interpretation of variable importance scores. As a result of redundancy effects because of total or partial, that often occurs during practice; the overall importance of the provided variable can be misguidedly small or highly misleading. This is because the same data is distributed within a couple of redundant variables which can be accounted for, within the total importance, several times.

It is, therefore, advisable to complement the interpretation with the variable scores being systematically decomposed. This will help immensely in understanding the reason why variables are important and how to detect redundancy conceivably.

Prejudice in Variable Importance

Variable importance is influenced immensely due to the masking effects, tree structure, and the impurity misestimations. These factors, later on, make the variable importance to deviate from possible results that are found in conditions referred to as asymptotic, that are in trees that are entirely randomized.

i. Partiality as a result of masking effects.

It has been known that decision trees that are constructed with randomization being too much tend to increase biases, respecting generalization error that compensation is involved as a result of variance decrease. Thus, K (which is a split variable for K>1) has to be adjusted accordingly to get the suitable trade-off.

Though there are instances, for example, if a variable selection is not random meaning, K>1, the masking effects that result in a bias about variable importance. Some branches are forced to entirely not built; therefore, some conditioning sets B $\in \mathcal{P}(V)$ are not considered. The result of such actions leads to random forests with the K as their parameter being tuned to make full use of accuracy that could yield variable importance that are one-sided or under- or overestimated.

Another instance can be having relevant variables that are null concerning its importance. Thus, it is indistinguishable from other irrelevant variables thus making the relevant variables dependent on some extraneous variables. This can be explained in the table below:

	X_1	$\sim N(0,1)$
	X_2	$\sim M(2)$
	X_3	$\sim M(4)$
	X_4	$\sim M(10)$
	X_5	$\sim M(20)$
null case	Y	$\sim B(0.5)$
power case	$Y|X_2 = 0$	$\sim B(0.5 - relevance)$
	$Y|X_2 = 1$	$\sim B(0.5 + relevance)$

The table shows the input variables that are independent random variables with:

- $N(0,1)$ the standard normal distribution

- $M(k)$ as the multinomial distribution with values ranging in $\{0,...,k-1\}$ and probabilities being equal

- $B(p)$ the binomial distribution

- When considering the null case, Y is dependent from $X_1,...,X_5$. Power case Y depends on X_2 value with the rest of the input variables being irrelevant.

ii. Bias because ofEmpirical Impurity Estimations

Analysis of variable importance has shown how asymptotic conditions, what identifies the impurity of an actual node are alleged to be acknowledged. But in practice, impurity measurements are afflicted with empirical misestimation bias. Node impurity misestimation is directly proportional to split variable cardinality, and the Number N_t samples that are used is inversely proportional to it. This results in a reduction in impurities that have been overestimated as the tree and the variables are largely due to some values. There are ramifications that occur afterward. The variable importance is affected by bias as the variables end up being cardinally higher and of more importance, which is a mistake.

Evaluating impurity on samples that are small eventually lead to mutual information being overestimated and variable importance being biased. More specifically, the high cardinality of variable leads to misestimations being large.

The ways to reduce the chances of this recurring is by halting early construction of tree or by making the leaves grow at a slower rate than size N, used on the learning set. To reduce over-estimations, do not use variable selection when evaluating variables' relevance.

In conclusion, trees that are built at maximum depth, larger than the relevant variables' number r, and stopping early construction of trees does not necessarily hinder us from identifying relevant variables.

iii. Threshold selection and Binary trees biases

In practice, we realize that random forests depend heavily on binary splits instead of multi-way splits. When it comes to impurity, it concludes to distinct and bonus data terms that earlier were not regarded due to;

i.   Binary splits detach the data that is a variable

ii. A similar variable is capable of being reused severally and its branch as well

These make the variable importance rely on split threshold assortment strategy. If a demanding theoretical framework lacks, the segment receives preliminary insights on the variable importance that can be found on binary decision trees. This might help in understanding their interpretation.

To understand this better, here's an example.

Toy classification problem that is made of ternary input variable X_1 and X_2 as the binary input variable with the two being ordered. It can be presumed that the data samples have been drawn equally defining the output as $Y = X_1 < X_2$ as a duplicate of Y. Concerning Y, the variables are informative, and they are expected for it to be a similar case with their importance. Exhaustive splits and randomized trees, there is the possibility of two equally probable decision trees to be built.

From:

$$Imp(X_1) = \frac{1}{2}I(X_1;Y) = \frac{1}{2}H(Y) = 0.459,$$
$$Imp(X_2) = \frac{1}{2}I(X_2;Y) = \frac{1}{2}H(Y) = 0.459.$$

You then get to make the samples that are equiprobable like shown below:

y	x_1	x_2
0	0	0
1	1	1
1	2	1

The randomized trees that are going to be built based on the samples above to get decision trees that are also equiprobable are going to be projected in this manner:

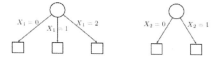

When binary splits and ETs that is K = 1, are used, resulting in varying decision trees:

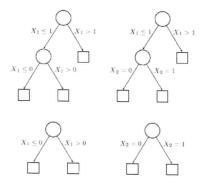

From the results above, the decision trees are being generated with a probability of (from left to right, top to bottom) 1/8, 1/8, 1/4 and 1/2. These results show that X_2 is of much importance than X_1.

To help with understanding the outcome above, the X_1 root node is split;showing that the binary roots have equal probability:

$t_L = X_1 \leqslant 0, t_R = X_1 > 0$ or $t_L = X_1 \leqslant 1, t_R = X_1 > 1$.

Previously, the child nodes that occurred were pure thus bringing to a standstill the construction process. In the most recent case, the corresponding $X_1 > 1$, which is the right child, is pure while the child on the left is not. In this particular node, the recurring partitioning goes on, so that the second binary split is simple on X_1 and X_2. The asymptotic conditions are in the binary trees as measured variable importance:

$$Imp(X_1) = \frac{2}{8}I(X_1 \leqslant 1; Y) + \frac{1}{8}P(X_1 \leqslant 1)I(X_1 \leqslant 0; Y|X_1 \leqslant 1) + \frac{1}{4}I(X_1 \leqslant 0; Y)$$
$$= 0.375$$
$$Imp(X_2) = \frac{1}{2}I(X_2; Y) + \frac{1}{8}P(X_1 \leqslant 1)I(X_2; Y|X_1 \leqslant 1)$$
$$= 0.541,$$

This differentiates them from importance that are gathered from the multi-way totally randomized trees. The importance is accountable for the conditioning sets as a result of binarization of split variables; which might also have some values that are found in the same variable. An example would be X_2 importance includes $I(X_2; Y|X_1 \leqslant 1)$, which translates to shared data between X_2 and Y; if X_1 is equivalent to 0 or 1. Conditioning sets are not considered in multi-way exhaustive splits due to the branches concurring to values that are singular only. Standard information terms like $I(X_1 \leqslant 1; Y)$ are taken into account by importance as well. It is best to understand that the randomized trees aren't accounted for due to the multi-way splits.

Variable importance are affected by binary splits through the threshold selection as the control of how binarization of primary variables occurs. Intermediate variables v are plausible in ETs, which result in combinatorial number on the additional impurity terms $I(X_j < v^*; Y|\cdot)$ and $I(\cdot; Y|X_j < v^*, \cdot)$ as this masks the rest.

A final example to show this is the variable importance for X_1 and X_2 that occur when cardinality increases $L = |X_1|$ for X_1 that can be seen on the toy problem. To redefine output as $Y = X_1 < L/2$, for $X_1 = \{0, ..., L - 1\}$, as X_2 is retained as binary variable that is classified as a duplicate of Y. Hypothetically speaking, in case the input samples are equiprobable, importance that are yielded by the randomized trees remain as before if they have multiway split. ETs are different though, L increases bring about more impurity terms that are new and are being taken into account when considering importance. Below, the figure does indicate the growth in cardinality of X_1 that results in the decrease of importance while simultaneously increasing X_2 importance. X_2 splitting always leads to child nodes that are pure which is not the case for X_1, when it is split randomly.

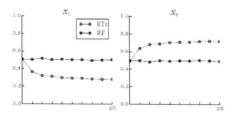

This shows the increase in cardinality of X_1 on the variable importance of X_1 and X_2.

Additional effects that are a result of binary splits generate variable importance from classical random forests. These are quite difficult to comprehend and elucidate as the information that contains several variables from a variety of categories. It is possible to identify the relevant variables with the data acquired, be cautious when clarifying importance amplitude. With the last example, there can be either misleadingly high or low due to the combinatorial effects. This is because of the possible ways variables can be binarized through the implementation of threshold selection mechanisms.

Summary

We would like to recommend you to look at the book Learning for Absolute Beginners: *A simple, Concise, and Complete Introduction to Supervised and Unsupervised Learning Algorithms*. This is with the aim of learning the basics of the following concepts as discussed in this book:

- Algorithmic types of Supervised learning

    - Bayesian Networks

    -Neural Networks

    -K-means algorithm

    -Perceptron

    -Logical regression

    - Boosting

- Step by step process of supervised learning

- Learning more about Back propagation algorithm

- Self-Organization Map (SOM)

- Advantages of SOM

- The difference between Supervised and Unsupervised Learning

Conclusion

Thank you for making it through to the end of *Machine Learning for Beginners: The Definitive Guide to Neural Networks, Random Forests, and Decision Trees*, let us hope that the information provided in this book was able to provide you with the skills in understanding how Neural Networks perform. We hope that you are now inspired in getting into learning the code and creating neural networks after understanding how they function. Reading this book is not the end of the road, it's just the beginning.

The next step you should take is to read more books that dig deeper into the code and building of networks that will enable you to implement in your application. You need to have a goal on how you intend to achieve this feat and even grow into this field progressively.

After you are done with this book, you will gain further understanding of the applications of Neural networks. Applications such as in fingerprint reading in cell phones and biometric systems, stock market prediction, medicine and other applications, will be a guide to understanding how you can start your applications. You will need to use this book as the foundation of the interesting world of applications.

Finally, if this book was useful in more than way, a review on Amazon will be much appreciated.